BEING CONFORMED TO THE
IMAGE OF CHRIST

UNLEASHED

ERIC MASON

LifeWay Press®
Nashville, Tennessee

Published by LifeWay Press® • © 2016 Eric Mason

ISBN 978-1-4300-3948-8 • Item 005717348

Dewey decimal classification: 248.84
Subject headings: CHRISTIAN LIFE / DISCIPLESHIP / SPIRITUAL LIFE

Scripture quotations are taken from The Holy Bible, English Standard Version® (ESV®), copyright © 2001 by Crossway, a publishing ministry of Good News Publishers. Used by permission. All rights reserved.

To order additional copies of this resource, write to LifeWay Resources Customer Service; One LifeWay Plaza; Nashville, TN 37234-0113; fax 615.251.5933; call toll free 800.458.2772; order online at *lifeway.com;* email *orderentry@lifeway.com;* or visit the LifeWay Christian Store serving you.

Printed in Canada

Groups Ministry Publishing • LifeWay Resources
One LifeWay Plaza • Nashville, TN 37234-0152

CONTENTS

ABOUT THE AUTHOR

Eric Mason is the founder and lead pastor of Epiphany Fellowship in Philadelphia, Pennsylvania. He lives in the heart of Philadelphia with his wife, Yvette; sons Immanuel, Nehemiah, and Ephraim; and daughter Amalyah. Pastor Mason is the founder and president of Thriving, an urban resource collaborative committed to developing leaders for ministry in an inner-city context. Pastor Mason has written three books: *Manhood Restored, Beat God to the Punch,* and *Unleashed.*

Pastor Mason has been graced by God to preach and teach at churches and conferences in the United States and abroad. He received a bachelor's degree in psychology from Bowie State University, a master of theology from Dallas Theological Seminary, and a doctoral degree from Gordon-Conwell Theological Seminary. Pastor Mason was first burdened as an undergraduate to go into full-time vocational service after trusting Christ.

Pastor Mason was then called to serve as the regional director of the Urban Schools Alternative at Oak Cliff Bible Fellowship. When he received the call to Philadelphia, Fellowship Bible Church in Little Rock, Arkansas, offered to train him in leadership and church planting. After his commissioning, Pastor Mason moved with his family to Philadelphia to plant Epiphany Fellowship.

HOW TO USE THIS STUDY

This Bible study provides a guided process for individuals and small groups to explore Scriptures that shape a Christian's view of spiritual growth, or sanctification. This study is divided into six key areas:

1. Grown by God Through the Gospel
2. Faith and Repentance
3. The Role of Suffering in Sanctification
4. Grown by the Word of God
5. Grown Through Prayer
6. Overcoming Strongholds

One week of Bible study is devoted to each of these topics, and each week is divided into three sections of personal study:

1. The Big Idea
2. Digging Deeper
3. Gospel Application

In these sections you'll find biblical teaching and interactive questions that will help you understand and apply the teaching.

In addition to the personal study, six group sessions are provided that are designed to spark gospel conversations around brief video teachings. Each group session is divided into three sections:

1. "Start" focuses participants on the topic of the session's video teaching.
2. "Watch" provides key Scriptures presented in the video and space to take notes.
3. "Respond" guides the group in a discussion of the video teaching.

If you want to go deeper in your study, you may want to read the book on which this Bible study is based. *Unleashed* (B&H Publishing) is ISBN 978-1-4336-8747-1.

TIPS FOR LEADING A SMALL GROUP

PRAYERFULLY PREPARE

Prepare for each group session with prayer. Ask the Holy Spirit to work through you and the group discussion as you point to Jesus each week through God's Word.

REVIEW the weekly material and group questions ahead of time.

PRAY for each person in the group.

MINIMIZE DISTRACTIONS

Do everything in your ability to help people focus on what's most important: connecting with God, with the Bible, and with one another.

CREATE A COMFORTABLE ENVIRONMENT. If group members are uncomfortable, they'll be distracted and therefore not engaged in the group experience.

TAKE INTO CONSIDERATION seating, temperature, lighting, refreshments, surrounding noise,and general cleanliness.

At best, thoughtfulness and hospitality show guests and group members they're welcome and valued in whatever environment you choose to gather. At worst, people may never notice your effort, but they're also not distracted.

INCLUDE OTHERS

Your goal is to foster a community in which people are welcome just as they are but encouraged to grow spiritually. Always be aware of opportunities to include and invite.

INCLUDE anyone who visits the group.

INVITE new people to join your group.

ENCOURAGE DISCUSSION

A good small-group experience has the following characteristics.

EVERYONE PARTICIPATES. Encourage everyone to ask questions, share responses, or read aloud.

NO ONE DOMINATES—NOT EVEN THE LEADER. Be sure your time speaking as a leader takes up less than half your time together as a group. Politely guide discussion if anyone dominates.

NOBODY IS RUSHED THROUGH QUESTIONS. Don't feel that a moment of silence is a bad thing. People often need time to think about their responses to questions they've just heard or to gain courage to share what God is stirring in their hearts.

INPUT IS AFFIRMED AND FOLLOWED UP. Make sure you point out something true or helpful in a response. Don't just move on. Build community with follow-up questions, asking how other people have experienced similar things or how a truth has shaped their understanding of God and the Scripture you're studying. People are less likely to speak up if they fear that you don't actually want to hear their answers or that you're looking for only a certain answer.

GOD AND HIS WORD ARE CENTRAL. Opinions and experiences can be helpful, but God has given us the truth. Trust Scripture to be the authority and God's Spirit to work in people's lives. You can't change anyone, but God can. Continually point people to the Word and to active steps of faith.

KEEP CONNECTING

Think of ways to connect with group members during the week. Participation during the group session is always improved when members spend time connecting with one another outside the group sessions. The more people are comfortable with and involved in one another's lives, the more they'll look forward to being together. When people move beyond being friendly to truly being friends who form a community, they come to each session eager to engage instead of merely attending.

ENCOURAGE GROUP MEMBERS with thoughts, commitments, or questions from the session by connecting through emails, texts, and social media.

BUILD DEEPER FRIENDSHIPS by planning or spontaneously inviting group members to join you outside your regularly scheduled group time for meals; fun activities; and projects around your home, church, or community.

GROWN BY GOD THROUGH THE GOSPEL

START

What's one thing you're looking forward to about this study or this time together as a group?

If someone asked you about the role of the gospel in your life, what would you say?

How often do you specifically think about the Holy Spirit? What questions do you have about His role in your life?

If you're a follower of Christ, you've had an encounter with the gospel. Most of us think of the gospel as the good news that saved us—and that's true—but that's not the whole story. We mustn't see our journey with Jesus as beginning and ending with a past moment. Rather, it's a continuous journey begun by God in the gospel, sustained by God in the gospel, and completed by God in the gospel. The gospel both begins and continues our journey with God.

Over the next six weeks we'll explore what it looks like to live lives that are both defined and propelled by the gospel. We'll discover how God uses the gospel to unleash His sanctifying power in our lives and to conform us to the image of Christ.

Read Romans 8:28-30 together as a group. Then watch video session I, in which Pastor Mason starts us on our journey by helping us understand how the gospel grows us in Christlikeness through the power of the Holy Spirit.

WATCH

If you abide in me, and my words abide in you, ask whatever you
wish, and it will be done for you. By this my Father is glorified,
that you bear much fruit and so prove to be my disciples.

JOHN 15:7-8

My beloved, as you have always obeyed, so now, not only as
in my presence but much more in my absence, work out your
own salvation with fear and trembling, for it is God who works
in you, both to will and to work for his good pleasure.

PHILIPPIANS 2:12-13

O foolish Galatians! Who has bewitched you? It was before your
eyes that Jesus Christ was publicly portrayed as crucified. Let
me ask you only this: Did you receive the Spirit by works of the
law or by hearing with faith? Are you so foolish? Having begun
by the Spirit, are you now being perfected by the flesh?

GALATIANS 3:1-3

Those whom he foreknew he also predestined to be
conformed to the image of his Son, in order that he
might be the firstborn among many brothers.

ROMANS 8:29

RESPOND

Pastor Mason covered a lot of ground as we began our study together. Let's begin with a simple question:

What stood out to you about Pastor Mason's teaching? How did the Lord speak to you?

We all have our view of salvation and its role in our lives. Pastor Mason helped us expand that view by explaining that the gospel speaks into every aspect of our lives throughout our lifetimes.

Why do you think it's so easy to view salvation as simply fire insurance from hell? What's the danger of this perspective?

Why do we so often view the fundamentals of our faith as something we leave behind?

One of the most important points Pastor Mason made in this video was that God is the One who grows us. Sanctification is primarily His work.

How does it affect your faith to know that God is the One who drives your spiritual growth?

Read John 15:7-8. In what ways can you more consistently abide in Christ? What does abiding look like for you?

What was the most challenging truth you heard Pastor Mason say?

In closing, pray and thank God not only for saving you but also for providing the means and the power to continue growing closer to Him and more like Him.

Complete the following three personal-study sections before the next group session. One section will focus on this week's big idea, the next section will dig deeper into Scripture, and the final section will focus on application.

THE BIG IDEA

Have you ever had that feeling you're just not growing spiritually? You're doing all the right things—attending church, reading your Bible, participating in a small group, and praying. Maybe you even attend extra Bible studies or conferences to help you grow. But you still find that overall, you feel spiritually stagnant. As a pastor, I can't tell you how many times I've heard people say some version of "I don't feel I'm growing." Many Christians wrestle with this issue, and the cause of this common feeling is a fundamental misunderstanding of what it takes to grow.

A young high-school basketball player was hungry to join the NBA. You could find him practicing to overcome his weaknesses, both before and after practice. His passion propelled him into a full scholarship at a major university. The stats he was putting on the board were unheard of for a freshman athlete at a school of that magnitude. Soon NBA scouts began to circle like hawks to get him. After arriving in the NBA, however, the young man seemed to lose his passion for the game. A large contract with guaranteed money had become an enabler for laziness. He could have been one of the top three players in the league if he'd retained his high-school work ethic. He needed to remember that the same practices that got him to the NBA were the same practices that would keep him there.

Many of us wonder why we're not growing in our spiritual lives. A lot of times it's because we think our growth depends only on us—that we have to work to achieve it all on our own. But it's the work of Jesus on the cross that brings us into a relationship with God, keeps us in a relationship with God, and grows us in our fellowship with God. Unlike the basketball player who had to rely on his own work ethic, not only to get him to the NBA but also to keep him there, the gospel functions in the spiritual life on our behalf. Now we still have skin in the game, as we'll talk about later, but it's the gospel and the work of the Holy Spirit in our lives that propel us to grow closer to the image of Christ.

That brings us to the big idea of this week's Bible study: God saves us and grows us through the gospel.

How would you describe the role of the gospel in your life? Record a few thoughts.

The purpose of this Bible study is to help you understand spiritual growth, or sanctification. The simplest way to view your sanctification is to see it as a constant process of being conformed to the image of Christ—growing more and more like Jesus.

Read Romans 8:28-30. What stands out to you about these verses?

What do these verses tell you about the relationship of your initial salvation (justification) to the actions that follow it?

It's essential that we view our spiritual lives as a process of being conformed to Jesus Christ, because whether or not we realize it, we're being conformed to something. Paul said it this way:

> Do not be conformed to this world, but be transformed by the
> renewal of your mind, that by testing you may discern what
> is the will of God, what is good and acceptable and perfect.
> **ROMANS 12:2**

In other words, if we aren't being conformed to the image of Christ, we're being conformed to the pattern of this world. There's no neutral option.

In what ways do you need to break your conformity to the world? List some.

What's one way the gospel—the saving message of Christ—could help you renew your mind?

If you had to assign a percentage that expresses the degree to which your heart is conformed to Christ, what would it be? Why did you choose that number?

A continuous return to the gospel will help us move our hearts and lives toward greater conformity to Christ. God begins this ongoing process when we're saved, and He completes it by the same means it began—through the gospel.

One of the most profound verses in the Bible on this subject is Romans 1:15: "I am eager to preach the gospel to you also who are in Rome." Paul's eagerness to preach the gospel to the believers in Rome wasn't because he thought they hadn't accepted the gospel but because he knew they needed to hear the gospel over and over. The same is true of believers today. We never graduate from our need to hear the gospel.

Paul wrote many letters to churches in the first century, mentioning the gospel more than 60 times in the letters of the New Testament. This fact is notable because Paul wrote these letters to groups of people who were already believers, as we saw in the previous example. Paul was constantly speaking about the gospel to believers. For example, Paul wrote this to the Philippian believers:

> ³I thank my God in all my remembrance of you, ⁴always in every prayer of mine for you all making my prayer with joy, ⁵because of your partnership in the gospel from the first day until now. ⁶And I am sure of this, that he who began a good work in you will bring it to completion at the day of Jesus Christ.
>
> **PHILIPPIANS 1:3-6**

Paul spoke of the Philippians as having partnered with him in the gospel from "the first day until now" (v. 5). What does this tell you about the role of the gospel in the lives of believers?

What does verse 6 tell you about the process of sanctification?

God justifies us through the gospel, and He sanctifies us with the gospel. Many of us adhere to faith-based justification (the idea that we're saved through faith), but we cling to a works-based notion of sanctification instead. In effect, we believe God saves us through the power of the gospel, but from that point forward we have to grow ourselves through our own power.

Read Ephesians 2:8. Briefly describe the gift of God referred to in this verse.

Hebrews 10:10 says, "By [God's] will we have been sanctified through the offering of the body of Jesus Christ once for all." The word *sanctified* in this verse is a perfect passive participle. Perfect tense means our sanctification is a completed work in the past. Consequently, our being set aside as holy by God has been done. A portion of our sanctification is already complete. The passive voice of the word *sanctified* points to the fact that it was done to us, not by us. Finally, the fact that the word *sanctified* is a participle means this state of sanctification describes our identity. We're continually being sanctified by God. Continual spiritual growth is part of what it means to be a Christian.

Scripture is clear that the gospel not only saves us but also grows us. It's also clear that the Holy Spirit plays a central role in our sanctification. We can't lose sight of that fact. If our theology is to be gospel-centered, we mustn't forget the Holy Spirit. He's the One who applies to us every component of the gospel. We don't grow and conform to the image of Christ in our own strength.

Sanctification mustn't be seen as separate from the gospel but as a part of it. It's an extension of the gospel. Read Paul's explanation:

> When the goodness and loving kindness of God our Savior appeared,
> he saved us, not because of works done by us in righteousness,
> but according to his own mercy, by the washing of regeneration
> and renewal of the Holy Spirit, whom he poured out on us richly
> through Jesus Christ our Savior, so that being justified by his grace
> we might become heirs according to the hope of eternal life.
> **TITUS 3:4-7**

According to this passage, what's the role of the Holy Spirit in our salvation?

Why do you think it's easy to forget about the Holy Spirit's role in our spiritual lives?

For too long the church (in some sectors) has had a reductionistic view of the Holy Spirit. In many cases He's understood simply as an idea from the Bible. We've ignored and therefore disconnected ourselves from the power of the Holy Spirit and His role in our sanctification.

Here are a few ways the Holy Spirit works in our lives to grow us closer to God.

1. THE SPIRIT CONVICTS US OF SIN, RIGHTEOUSNESS, AND JUDGMENT.

> When he comes, he will convict the world concerning sin and righteousness and judgment: concerning sin, because they do not believe in me; concerning righteousness, because I go to the Father, and you will see me no longer; concerning judgment, because the ruler of this world is judged.
>
> **JOHN 16:8-11**

2. THE SPIRIT OPENS OUR HEARTS TO THE GOSPEL TO CONFESS JESUS.

> I want you to understand that no one speaking in the Spirit of God ever says "Jesus is accursed!" and no one can say "Jesus is Lord" except in the Holy Spirit.
>
> **1 CORINTHIANS 12:3**

3. THE SPIRIT REGENERATES AND RENEWS US THROUGH THE GOSPEL.

> He saved us, not because of works done by us in righteousness, but according to his own mercy, by the washing of regeneration and renewal of the Holy Spirit.
>
> **TITUS 3:5**

4. THE SPIRIT SEALS AND SECURES US IN THE FAITH.

> You also ... were sealed with the promised Holy Spirit, who is the guarantee of our inheritance until we acquire possession of it, to the praise of his glory.
>
> **EPHESIANS 1:13-14**

> ... who by God's power are being guarded through faith
> for a salvation ready to be revealed in the last time.
> **I PETER 1:5**

From leading us to faith in Jesus Christ, to initially saving us, to maintaining our faith in Jesus Christ as He sanctifies us, to preserving our faith in the blessed hope that He will glorify us, we need the power of the Holy Spirit. He's the wind that turns the turbines of our souls, lives, and ministries. And of course, as we'll see throughout this study, He causes us to grow into conformity to the image of Christ.

In your own words, record your best understanding of the word *sanctification*.

The Holy Spirit sanctified us at salvation, yet He continues to work to conform us to Christ's image. Holiness isn't something we have to work for or achieve on our own. The Holy Spirit draws us to Christ through the gospel in the first place, and the Spirit grows us toward spiritual maturity through that same gospel as we follow Christ.

Finish this section of your study by praying the following prayer.

Holy Spirit, I thank You that You know me. I thank You that You love me in spite of the many times I overlook Your role in my life. I thank You that You see me for who I am and seek me in spite of my many sins and failures. Holy Spirit, I thank You that You're the one who drew me to Christ through the gospel and brought me into a relationship with Him. I thank You that You're constantly preaching the gospel to me again and again so that I can be transformed by it and become more and more like Jesus. Holy Spirit, I pray that You'll refine me, smooth out my rough edges, and mold and shape me into Christ's image. I ask You to work through the details of my daily life to make me the person God intends for me to be. I submit myself to You and Your sanctifying work. Amen.

God saves us and grows us through the GOSPEL.
#UNLEASHED

DIGGING DEEPER

When we're drawn toward God and place our faith in the work of His Son, Paul tells us we become new creations:

> If anyone is in Christ, he is a new creation.
> The old has passed away; behold, the new has come.
> **2 CORINTHIANS 5:17**

As new creations, we have a new identity. The old is dead, and the new has come. We have new desires and new natures. And it's this new identity, through the gospel, that's continually being shaped in greater likeness to the image of Christ.

Colossians 3:1-17 describes this new nature and our response to it. Read this passage and notice the progression of sanctification that Paul described. How does each section speak to being shaped in the likeness of Christ?

Verses 1-4   Verses 5-11   Verses 12-17

Throughout the New Testament Paul distinguished between a believer's old and new identities. Read the following verses and record your answers to these questions: What's the common thread? What's the Spirit's role? What's our role?

> We know that our old self was crucified with him
> in order that the body of sin might be brought to nothing,
> so that we would no longer be enslaved to sin.
> **ROMANS 6:6**

> Put off your old self, which belongs to your former manner of
> life and is corrupt through deceitful desires, and to be renewed
> in the spirit of your minds, and to put on the new self, created
> after the likeness of God in true righteousness and holiness.
> **EPHESIANS 4:22-24**

> I say, walk by the Spirit, and you will not gratify the desires of the flesh. For the
> desires of the flesh are against the Spirit, and the desires of the Spirit are against
> the flesh, for these are opposed to each other, to keep you from doing the things
> you want to do. But if you are led by the Spirit, you are not under the law.
>
> **GALATIANS 5:16-18**

Record your thoughts below.

SPIRITUAL MILK VS. SOLID FOOD

When we place our trust in Christ for the first time, we take a step onto a lifelong path of spiritual growth and maturity. At that moment we're spiritual babies. When children are born, they're born fully human—as human as they're ever going to be. On the other hand, being newborn humans, babies are unable to maximize their full potential. Walking, talking, eating on their own—all the potential for these activities exist in the child, but development is necessary for that potential to be realized.

The same thing is true of our sanctification as believers. We're fully justified when we respond to the gospel and place our trust in Christ, but we're unable to maximize our full spiritual potential. We have to be sanctified and grow up in our faith in order to be mature believers. God has to continuously shape and mold us into the image of Christ throughout our lives. Peter talked about this idea in one of his letters, encouraging his readers to grow from spiritual infants into spiritual adults:

> Like newborn infants, long for the pure spiritual milk,
> that by it you may grow up into salvation.
>
> **I PETER 2:2**

The apostle Paul also spoke of spiritual infancy in his first letter to the Corinthians, stating that it was necessary for him to begin his teaching ministry in Corinth with spiritual milk rather than spiritual solid food. He also lamented that the Corinthian Christians were still dependent on that spiritual milk when they should have long moved on to solid food:

> I, brothers, could not address you as spiritual people,
> but as people of the flesh, as infants in Christ. I fed you
> with milk, not solid food, for you were not ready for it. And
> even now you are not yet ready, for you are still of the flesh.
>
> **I CORINTHIANS 3:1-3**

In what areas of your life are you still feeding on spiritual milk (more elementary teachings from Scripture)?

What practical steps can you take to move on to solid spiritual food (a deeper understanding of the Christian life)?

The writer of Hebrews also reprimanded his readers for not having matured beyond their spiritual infancy. Notice the similarities between this text and Paul's words to the Corinthians:

> Though by this time you ought to be teachers, you need someone to teach you again the basic principles of the oracles of God. You need milk, not solid food, for everyone who lives on milk is unskilled in the word of righteousness, since he is a child. But solid food is for the mature, for those who have their powers of discernment trained by constant practice to distinguish good from evil. Therefore let us leave the elementary doctrine of Christ and go on to maturity.
> **HEBREWS 5:12–6:1**

When you think about your past spiritual journey, what kinds of beliefs, attitudes, or behaviors represented spiritual milk for you? What did you need to fully grasp in the early days of your faith in Christ?

How has the gospel propelled you forward from your spiritual infancy?
According to the writer of Hebrews, how can we continue to eat spiritual solid food and not revert to the milk of our spiritual infancy?

God has a dynamic process in place by which He ushers the redeemed from spiritual infancy to spiritual maturity. God's work in us is always in motion, but the question is, Are we submissive to the process of His sanctifying work in our lives?

Paul described this process in his letter to the Corinthians:

> We do not lose heart. Though our outer self is wasting away, our inner self is being renewed day by day.
> **1 CORINTHIANS 4:16**

The process of sanctification is often referred to as progressive sanctification because it's an ongoing effort. We don't cause our own growth, but the Spirit grows us as we pursue the holiness of Christ and access the means God makes available for us to grow. Therefore, God is sanctifying us, but our role is to submit to His sanctifying work. Look at Paul's words to the Philippians on this subject:

> My beloved, as you have always obeyed, so now, not only as in my presence but much more in my absence, work out your own salvation with fear and trembling, for it is God who works in you, both to will and to work for his good pleasure.
> **PHILIPPIANS 2:12-13**

What's our role in our own sanctification, according to these verses?

What's God's role?

What we're discussing is of utmost importance for the believer. It's important because God's sanctifying work in us extends to every aspect of our lives. Every aspect of our lives means conformity to Christ in every way. That's why Paul could say, "All things work together for good" (Rom. 8:28) in the context of God's predestined work of conforming us to the divine image. It isn't something we as humans begin or sustain.

Jesus is the goal of the Christian life. Every sector of our lives is a harvest field for the work of God to make us holy in Jesus. Just as a gardener uses rakes, shovels, plows, fertilizer, and pruning devices, every aspect of this world is a means of grace for God to make us look like the Lord Jesus Christ. The circumstances and experiences of our lives are tools for conforming us to His image.

In John 15:1 Jesus called God the Father "the vinedresser," or the gardener. The Father as our gardener is the visionary leader of our sanctification. In the same passage Jesus called Himself the vine, the source of all the ways we grow. And the Spirit was introduced as the leader who harvests our sanctification (see John 14–17). The Spirit guides us into the means of conformity to Christ, making sure the life of Jesus and the direction of the Father are connected and applied to our lives. The Spirit applies the gospel to every area of our lives. Therefore, the triune God works in concert together for our growth.

PAST, PRESENT, AND FUTURE SANCTIFICATION

Scripture is clear that those who've repented and believed in the good news of Jesus Christ have been sanctified, are being sanctified, and will be sanctified. This is a past, present, and future process. All this is done by a believer's faith in the gospel and by the activity of the Holy Spirit.

PAST: WE'VE BEEN SANCTIFIED

> You were washed, you were sanctified, you were justified in the
> name of the Lord Jesus Christ and by the Spirit of our God.
> **I CORINTHIANS 6:11**

Circle the three things the Holy Spirit does for us, according to this verse. What does it mean to you to know God did this for you?

PRESENT: WE'RE BEING SANCTIFIED

> Are you so foolish? Having begun by the Spirit,
> are you now being perfected by the flesh?
> **GALATIANS 3:3**

Paul asked this pointed rhetorical question of the Galatian believers, implying they'd been trying to achieve their spiritual growth on their own without the power of the Spirit.

List a few ways you've tried to sanctify yourself, as well as the results.

FUTURE: WE'LL BE SANCTIFIED

> May the God of peace himself sanctify you completely,
> and may your whole spirit and soul and body be kept
> blameless at the coming of our Lord Jesus Christ.
> **I THESSALONIANS 5:23**

> When Christ had offered for all time a single sacrifice for sins,
> he sat down at the right hand of God, waiting from that time until
> his enemies should be made a footstool for his feet. For by a single
> offering he has perfected for all time those who are being sanctified.
> **HEBREWS 10:12-14**

Why does God sanctify us in the present and future? Why do you think sanctification is an ongoing process instead of a one-time action at the moment we're justified?

Take a few moments and reflect on your past, present, and future sanctification—things God has done, is doing, and will do in your life to make you holier. First list a few things God has done in your life in the past to sanctify you.

List a few things God is currently doing in your life to make you more like Christ.

Finally, record some things you hope God does to sanctify you in the future.

Close this section by asking yourself some honest questions:
☐ How much do I care about God's sanctifying me?
☐ How often have I asked God to make me look more like Jesus?
☐ What's at stake if I don't fully seek the Lord for my sanctification?

Now pray the prayer below, inserting into the blanks the things God has done in your life, is doing in your life, and you hope He will do in your life.

Holy Spirit, I'm depending on You to conform me to the image of Christ. I thank You for the sanctifying work You've done in my life in the past. I thank You specifically for the ways You _____. I also thank You for the ways You're working in my life right now. Help me be submissive to that process and trust that You're molding and shaping me into the image of Christ. Thank You for currently leading me through _____. Holy Spirit, I also ask that You'll continue to sanctify me in the future. Make me holier throughout my life by _____. I pray that You'll apply the gospel to every area of my life and prepare my heart to fully cooperate with that process. In Christ's name, amen.

God has a dynamic process in place by which He ushers the redeemed from spiritual infancy to spiritual maturity.
#UNLEASHED

GOSPEL APPLICATION

Up to this point we've focused primarily on God's role in our sanctification, specifically the way the Holy Spirit applies the gospel to our lives and conforms us to the image of Christ. However, that's not the whole story. It's vitally important that we also see ourselves as active participants in desiring God and growing in Christlikeness. And it's not an easy task. Sanctification is a victorious struggle—victorious in that Jesus has secured our sanctification but a struggle in that we're called to actively pursue holiness.

Indicate on the scale the degree to which you actively pursue holiness.

1	2	3	4	5
Never				Daily

What does that pursuit look like for you? How are you actively participating in the Holy Spirit's work in your life?

When we address this topic, we tend to fall on one of two opposite poles on a spectrum. Some believers talk about holiness being rooted in the character and action of God, but they never speak of how we pursue holiness in our daily lives. This way of thinking can lead us to become spiritually stagnant because we're always waiting for God to act.

At the other end of the scale are people who do pragmatic works that seek to grow themselves, but they don't root their actions in what God has done for them in the Lord Jesus Christ and through the Holy Spirit. This kind of thinking can lead to a brand of self-help Christianity or a theology of works righteousness in which people put forth a lot of self-effort to be better Christians.

Do you tend to rely on God for your spiritual growth or to make proactive choices to change your life? How has this approach affected your spiritual life?

What are the dangers of not having a balanced perspective—of either trying to achieve sanctification through our own efforts or not doing enough?

How can you have a more balanced perspective of relying on God's sovereignty over your spiritual growth while still taking responsibility for your part in the process?

Let's look at Philippians 2:12-13 again, this time from the vantage point of applying the gospel to our lives. These verses make a paradoxical statement about spiritual growth:

> My beloved, as you have always obeyed, so now, not only as
> in my presence but much more in my absence, work out your
> own salvation with fear and trembling, for it is God who works
> in you, both to will and to work for his good pleasure.
> **PHILIPPIANS 2:12-13**

Paul called the Philippian church to obedience motivated by God's work in them, not by Paul's presence with them. Paul wanted these Christians to know that he didn't work in them, but God did. In their pursuit of holiness, he called them to work *out* their salvation, not *for* their salvation. This is the paradox: we work out our salvation even though God is the One who ultimately sanctifies us. In other words, we're to be diligent in pursuing the means to look more and more like Christ while doing so with fear and trembling—that is, reverence for God and trust in the fact that He's supervising and directing the process.

In what way do you see the gospel in these verses from Philippians?

Notice Paul's words about obedience. How do you think most people view obedience—as positive or negative? What role does obedience to God play in our sanctification?

If you had to sum up the process of sanctification in one sentence based on these verses alone, what would it be? Record that sentence here.

The paradox of sanctification—that it's primarily God's work but also includes our active participation—means one way we can make an effort in our sanctification is to more fully and consistently yield to the Holy Spirit's work in our lives. We need to get out of the way of what He wants to do through us, at the same time working to become a more and more useful vessel for His purposes.

Ultimately, we want to be so yielded to the Lord and so open to be used by Him that we're filled with the Holy Spirit, as the apostle Paul wrote about in Ephesians 5. There Paul was encouraging the Ephesian Christians to behave in a certain way and not to fall back into their old way of life before they knew Christ. He wrote:

> Do not be foolish, but understand what the will
> of the Lord is. And do not get drunk with wine,
> for that is debauchery, but be filled with the Spirit.
> **EPHESIANS 5:17-18**

The remarkable thing about this text is that the phrase "Be filled with the Spirit" (v. 18) is a command. It's something God instructs us to do. We don't have a choice about it. That means we're supposed to actively seek being filled with the Spirit. However, the verb "be filled" is in the passive voice, which means it's something that happens to us, not by us. God is the One filling us with the Spirit. The verb is also present tense, which in Greek, the original language of the New Testament, indicated that we should be filled with the Spirit in a continual, ongoing way. Being filled with the Holy Spirit should be a constant pursuit by any believer.

If God commands you to be filled with the Holy Spirit, yet it's something only He can do for you, how can you obey that commandment? What practical step(s) can you take to be filled with the Spirit?

In Romans 5:5 Paul elaborated by saying our ability to be filled with the Holy Spirit derives from a deliberate act of love on God's part: "God's love has been poured into our hearts through the Holy Spirit who has been given to us."

Have you ever thought about the Holy Spirit as a gift of God's love to us? What does this truth tell you about God?

As we seek to live out the gospel in our lives, the Holy Spirit makes that possible. We're justified in the first place through the power of the Spirit, and we're made to look more and more like Christ through the ongoing, active, sanctifying work of the Spirit. The Holy Spirit applies the gospel to every aspect of our lives, and He teaches us what that application looks like in our lives day to day.

We're not smart enough, insightful enough, observant enough, godly enough, wise enough, or self-aware enough to fully grasp the power of the gospel every day and to know how to apply it to our lives. We need the Holy Spirit to guide us through the process of spiritual growth. But this means we need to work to give ourselves every opportunity for the Spirit to speak. We can't possibly hear from God if we aren't exhausting the tools we've been given like prayer and the study and memorization of His Word, thus allowing the Spirit to speak through those means.

In Romans 8:26-28 Paul wrote about this process and the way the Holy Spirit guides us:

> The Spirit helps us in our weakness. For we do not know what
> to pray for as we ought, but the Spirit himself intercedes for
> us with groanings too deep for words. And he who searches
> hearts knows what is the mind of the Spirit, because the Spirit
> intercedes for the saints according to the will of God. And we
> know that for those who love God all things work together
> for good, for those who are called according to his purpose.
>
> **ROMANS 8:26-28**

Carefully read this passage one more time and record what the Holy Spirit does that helps conform you to the image of Christ.

How would the actions of the Holy Spirit, as described in this passage, help you better apply the gospel in your life?

What's the role of God's will in our sanctification?

We never get beyond the gospel in our Christian life. We never graduate to something more "advanced." The gospel isn't the first step in a "stairway of truths"; rather, it's more like the hub in a wheel of truth. The gospel isn't just the ABCs of Christianity but also the A–Z. The gospel isn't just the minimum required doctrine necessary to enter the Kingdom but also the way we make all progress in the Kingdom.[1]

We could never grasp and apply the gospel to our lives without the power of the Holy Spirit. So we never graduate from the gospel, and we make no progress without the Spirit's presence and guidance in our lives.

If we're to be sanctified—conformed to the image of Christ—then we always need to hold the gospel high in our lives. We need to understand that it's not only the power that justifies us in the first place but also God's tool to grow us toward spiritual maturity from that point forward. And the best part about it is that God Himself—God the Holy Spirit—does the heavy lifting in that process. We just need to submit ourselves to His will and find ways to actively participate in what the Holy Spirit is doing to make us look more and more like Jesus in our words, our attitudes, and our actions.

Finish this week's study with this prayer.

God, I know sometimes I don't view the gospel with the right lenses. I confess that I've regularly relegated it to a dusty corner of my faith. Sometimes I think of the gospel as simply something that saved me and that I need to tell other people. Help me, Lord, by the power of Your indwelling Holy Spirit, to grasp Your majesty and the life-changing power of the gospel: both the power to justify and the power to sanctify. Lord, help me be sensitive to ways You're moving in my life and ways Your Spirit is leading me to apply the gospel in my daily life. Help me be a joyful, active participant in that process, even if it requires pain or sacrifice. Help me view Your Spirit's role in my life as a gift of love from You. Father, help me never lose sight of the ongoing work of Your love, Your gospel, and Your Spirit to make me like Jesus. Grow me, Lord, through Your gospel and by the power of Your Spirit. Amen.

1. Timothy Keller, "The Centrality of the Gospel," *The Movement Newsletter,* Redeemer Presbyterian Church.

Sanctification is the victorious struggle—victorious in that Jesus has secured our sanctification but a struggle in that we're called to actively pursue holiness.
#UNLEASHED

FAITH AND REPENTANCE

START

Welcome to session 2 of *Unleashed*. Open the group session by asking participants to discuss the following questions.

As you completed this week's personal study, what did the Lord show you? How did He speak to you?

What's your view of repentance? What does it mean to you, and what does it look like to practice it?

What's the role of faith in repentance? How are faith and repentance related?

One of the most prevalent themes in the New Testament letters is false teaching. Paul and the other early Christian leaders continually battled against false teachers who distorted the gospel of Jesus Christ. If a few key ingredients are missing, the message of salvation doesn't resemble the gospel of Jesus Christ. Faith and repentance are two of those ingredients. Without them the gospel takes on a very different, unbiblical shape. In the same way the early churches were susceptible to false teaching, our own personal faith is vulnerable to distortion if it doesn't incorporate biblical repentance.

Today we'll hear Pastor Mason discuss the relationship between faith and repentance, highlighting the way those two ingredients work together for our sanctification.

Watch video session 2, in which Pastor Mason brings clarity to the often misunderstood subject of repentance.

WATCH

Jesus came into Galilee, proclaiming the gospel of God,
and saying, "The time is fulfilled, and the kingdom
of God is at hand; repent and believe in the gospel."

MARK 1:14-15

If we say we have no sin, we deceive ourselves, and the truth is not in us.

1 JOHN 1:8

Whoever conceals his transgressions will not prosper,
but he who confesses and forsakes them will obtain mercy.

PROVERBS 28:13

I know my transgressions,
and my sin is ever before me.

PSALM 51:3

If we confess our sins, he is faithful and just to forgive us
our sins and to cleanse us from all unrighteousness.

1 JOHN 1:9

Faith is the assurance of things hoped for,
the conviction of things not seen.

HEBREWS 11:1

Now to him who is able to strengthen you according
to my gospel and the preaching of Jesus Christ.

ROMANS 16:25

RESPOND

In this video session Pastor Mason showed us that the true biblical gospel is rooted in the concepts of faith and repentance.

What stood out to you in this video session?

How did Pastor Mason's description of repentance compare with popular ideas of what it means to repent?

Pastor Mason used King David as an example of someone who knew the value of repentance.

What does it mean to you to know that a prominent hero of the Old Testament admitted his sins and actively turned from them?

As Pastor Mason said, repentance is coupled with faith.

How do you believe your faith in God enables you to have a repentant heart?

Have you ever experienced the freedom of repentance? What did that experience teach you about God and your life as a Christ follower?

What was the most challenging truth you heard Pastor Mason say?

In closing, pray and thank God for His willingness to forgive and restore us when we repent of our sins. Also thank Him for sustaining our faith through the gospel, enabling us to have repentant hearts.

Complete the following three personal-study sections before the next group session. One section will focus on this week's big idea, the next section will dig deeper into Scripture, and the final section will focus on application.

THE BIG IDEA

I consider myself a pound-cake aficionado. I enjoy the crustiness of the top, fresh out of the oven, as well as the moist interior. There isn't anything like a freshly baked pound cake to bless the soul. One time my wife and I went to some folks' home and had a delectable meal. When dessert was served, to my surprise—but not to my dismay—it was pound cake. It came fresh out of the oven, and I was ready to be anointed by its presence. However, when this delight touched my tongue, it instantly became obvious that something was deeply wrong. I again asked our hosts what type of cake it was, and again they replied, "Pound cake." They then added, "Oh, you recognize the difference?" My mind screamed, *Yes!* They explained, "We substituted applesauce for the pound of butter."

I felt I'd been bamboozled. You see, pound cake isn't pound cake without the pound of butter. I want it at least once or twice a year—not too often. But when I have it, I want the real deal. My hosts didn't realize that in changing that one ingredient, they'd changed the identity of the cake from pound cake to something altogether different.

Just as one ingredient altered that pound cake, if one ingredient of the gospel is removed, it changes the identity of what we believe. If we take repentance or faith out of the gospel, the integrity of what we profess is altered.

That's the big idea of this week's Bible study: faith and repentance are two required ingredients of receiving the gospel and growing in it. Sanctification is rooted in faith and repentance. Our spiritual growth can be stunted if we don't consistently repent of our sin and believe in Christ's work on our behalf to plant and sustain us in the ongoing, transforming power of the gospel.

How would you define *faith?*

What do you think of when you hear the word *repentance?*

Does the word *repentance* have a positive or negative connotation for you? Why?

REPENTANCE

Let's start by exploring the idea of repentance. *Repentance* can be defined as "the conscious turning of the regenerate person away from sin and toward God in a complete change of living, which reveals itself in a new way of thinking, feeling, and willing."[1]

Repentance is literally a change of mind—not about individual plans, intentions, or beliefs but rather a change in the whole person from a sinful course of action to God. The Gospel of Mark records Jesus' first sermon. In it Jesus said:

> The time is fulfilled, and the kingdom of God
> is at hand; repent and believe in the gospel.
> **MARK 1:15**

Jesus said He wanted people to change their minds about their lives, what God is like, His kingdom, and the Messiah's coming. He wanted them to embrace His viewpoint. Repentance is the work of God by which He acts on sinners, through the Holy Spirit, so that we can realize our sin and embrace the truth of the gospel.

Why do you think Jesus spoke about repentance at the beginning of His ministry? Why was this idea a fundamental part of His message?

In what areas of your life do you need to repent? How can you consciously turn from those behaviors or attitudes?

What does repentance actually look like? What are the steps we can take toward repentance? In short, repentance is the ongoing process of confession, turning from sin, and faith. Let's talk a bit about each of those, and we'll expand on them in the next two sections of this week's study.

CONFESSION

Confession is communicating to God that we've rebelled against Him, without attempting to shift blame. In other words, we own the full extent of our sin. David exemplified this posture in the remarkably honest and contrite Psalm 51:

Have mercy on me, O God,
    according to your steadfast love;
according to your abundant mercy
    blot out my transgressions.
Wash me thoroughly from my iniquity,
    and cleanse me from my sin!
For I know my transgressions,
    and my sin is ever before me.
Against you, you only, have I sinned
    and done what is evil in your sight,
so that you may be justified in your words
    and blameless in your judgment.
PSALM 51:1-4

In verse 3 David said, "I know my transgressions." The Hebrew word for *know* here is a term of intimacy. David said "my," not "my and Bathsheba's." He confessed to God about his own sin, not anyone else's. He wasn't blind to the reality of his sin. He didn't minimize or explain it. He was intimately knowledgeable of his sin, and he confessed it.

What else do you notice about the previous passage? What does it teach you about the value of confession?

What does this passage teach you about the way to confess your sins to God?

David was one of the greatest leaders in the Bible. One thousand years later during the time of Christ, David was a hero to the Jews. It was considered an honor for anyone to be his descendant. Many of the people in the crowds following Jesus referred to Him as Son of David, which was a regal title for the promised Messiah. But David, this great hero of God, was no saint. He needed to confess his sins just like the rest of us. When he did, God forgave and restored him.

You and I can't repent unless we're generally and specifically clear on the sinfulness of our sin. Generally, we know we're sinners because the Bible says so. But a general knowledge of sin isn't confession; even some unbelievers know they're sinners generally but would never admit to specific sins they've committed against God and others. We must get comfortable with confessing our specific sins if we're going to truly repent.

What's the hardest time you've ever had in confessing a sin?

Do you find it harder to admit your sin to someone close to you or to someone you don't know very well?

Do you find it difficult to ask God for forgiveness? Why or why not?

TURNING FROM SIN

After confession the next stage of repentance is turning from our sin. This is a difficult step, but the good news is that we don't have to do all this on our own. Remember, God is the One who does the heavy lifting in our sanctification. Christ Himself actually frees us by faith to wholeheartedly abandon our sin. According to 2 Peter 1:

> His divine power has granted to us all things that pertain to life
> and godliness, through the knowledge of him who called us to
> his own glory and excellence, by which he has granted to us his
> precious and very great promises, so that through them you may
> become partakers of the divine nature, having escaped from
> the corruption that is in the world because of sinful desire.
>
> **2 PETER 1:3-4**

Through Jesus we've already escaped the corruption that's in the world through sinful desires.

When God makes us aware of our sin, but we still choose to walk in it, we can't grow in spiritual intimacy with God. Our growth is stunted. Yet a believer has assurance of hope for a continued relationship with God because Christ gives us the power to leave our sin behind. Only by confessing our sin, then turning away from it and abandoning it, can we unleash the power of sanctification in our lives.

In what ways do you believe your spiritual growth been stunted by an unwillingness to turn from sin?

List three sins you've been able to successfully turn away from.

How is your relationship with God different now that those behaviors are no longer a habitual part of your life?

How can leaving those sins behind motivate you to abandon other sins?

FAITH

Loyalty is the relational emulsifier of male friendships. Generally speaking, there's an unspoken rule among men that if I'm wrong, tell me alone. Don't publicly agree with others who aren't in our crew. Loyalty is the fraternal bond of human masculinity. For men, the stronger the loyalty, the deeper the friendship.

In a similar way, faith is the emulsifier that God uses to keep us connected to the gospel. It's faith that initially connects us to Jesus. And because of God's grace and the power of the Spirit's wooing us, God guards our salvation in Jesus in eternity. Faith keeps us connected to Jesus throughout the sanctification process and forever.

One of the most famous Scripture passages on faith is Proverbs 3:5-6:

> Trust in the LORD with all your heart,
>   and do not lean on your own understanding.
> In all your ways acknowledge him,
>   and he will make straight your paths.
> **PROVERBS 3:5-6**

Having faith in Christ means trusting in God's character and His promises—believing God will save us through Christ and will guard our salvation. Putting our faith in Christ is a perfect illustration of this Proverbs passage, because to believe a man died on a cross, came back to life, and ascended into heaven requires a full yielding of the heart to God. Responding to the gospel is the ultimate act of trusting the Lord with all our heart and not leaning on our own understanding. Paul wrote:

> The word of the cross is folly to those who are perishing,
> but to us who are being saved it is the power of God.
> **I CORINTHIANS 1:18**

The word *folly* is a translation of the Greek word *moria,* which is often translated as *foolishness* or *nonsense*. In other words, the gospel requires full trust in God—genuine faith. We can't believe in the gospel of Jesus Christ without God's drawing us to Him and without a heart that's full of faith.

When you first came to Christ, what did it feel like to put your faith in Him?

If you've been a Christian for a while, record a few seasons in your life when your faith was strong.

Why do you think your faith was strong during those times?

What were some times when you felt your faith falter?

Why do you think that happened?

To grow closer to God and grow in conformity to Christ's likeness, we must continually repent of sin. That's an integral part of the Christian faith and a prerequisite to knowing God in an authentic, intimate way. We have to confess our sins, follow through by turning away from them, and continually stoke the fires of our faith as we walk through our lives.

Finish this section by asking God to speak to your heart on this issue of repentance and to teach you what you need to hear. Ask God to search your heart for sin and make that sin known to you. Confess those sins, turn away from them, and by faith trust in His promises.

1. Anthony A. Hoekema, *Saved by Grace* (Grand Rapids, MI: Eerdmans, 1989), 127.

> *If we take repentance or faith out of the gospel, the integrity of what we profess is altered.*
> **#UNLEASHED**

DIGGING DEEPER

One of my favorite songs is "Running Back to You" by Commissioned. The song describes God's grace in drawing someone back to Himself. It's an ode to repentance.

In college I remember smoking a drug in my car while driving. A Christian friend had given me a cassette tape with Christian songs on it. I was a believer, but I wrestled with a ton of issues. While in the car, I pressed play without knowing what I was doing. I heard the lyrics of "Running Back to You" and began to weep bitterly as I sensed my need to repent. God used this song to call me to repentance. This and many other key moments placed me on an intentional sanctifying trajectory.

Have you ever experienced a moment when God spoke to you and highlighted your need for repentance?

Have you ever felt God deliberately correcting your course? What was that like, and how did you respond?

Repentance is also meant to give witness to God's grace—not just to you personally but to others around you who see the transformation take place in your life. Repentance is both edifying and evangelistic, ministerial and missional, worship and a witness. Here are some other helpful definitions of *repentance*:

1. To feel remorse, contrition, or self-reproach for what one has done or failed to do; to be contrite
2. To feel such regret for past conduct as to change one's mind about it; to repent of intemperate behavior
3. To make a change for the better as a result of remorse or contrition for one's sins

Which of these definitions resonates most with where you are in life? Explain.

Let's continue this week's study by digging deeper into the three elements of repentance we've already identified—confession, turning from sin, and faith—in order to understand their importance in our ongoing growth toward Christlikeness.

CONFESSION

Sometimes the hardest part of healing a relationship is saying the first few words—simply broaching the subject and beginning the process of admitting we're wrong. It's the hardest step and sometimes feels impossible, but often it's nowhere nearly as difficult as we expected, and we experience a huge sense of relief when the confession is over. This is true of many human relationships (especially marriage), but it's also true of our relationship with God.

Read this passage from Psalm 32:

> ¹Blessed is the one whose transgression is forgiven,
>   whose sin is covered.
> ²Blessed is the man against whom the LORD counts no iniquity,
>   and in whose spirit there is no deceit.
> ³For when I kept silent, my bones wasted away
>   through my groaning all day long.
> ⁴For day and night your hand was heavy upon me;
>   my strength was dried up as by the heat of summer.
> ⁵I acknowledged my sin to you,
>   and I did not cover my iniquity;
> I said, "I will confess my transgressions to the LORD,"
>   and you forgave the iniquity of my sin.
>
> **PSALM 32:1-5**

What kind of encouragement might the psalmist's words give to someone who is under conviction of sin?

This passage calls a person blessed if their sins have been forgiven or covered (see v. 1). In what ways have you been blessed by God's forgiveness of your sins?

What's the consequence of not confessing our sins (see vv. 3-4)?

TURNING FROM SIN

One of the most powerful passages on the role of confession in repentance is this:

> Whoever conceals his transgressions will not prosper,
> but he who confesses and forsakes them will obtain mercy.
>
> **PROVERBS 28:13**

The word *conceals* is the opposite of confession. It means refusing to acknowledge sin in confession or perhaps rationalizing sin. In contrast, consider the person who both confesses and turns away from the sin. To confess sin means to acknowledge sin, to say the same thing about sin that God does.

Which sins in your life do you have trouble acknowledging as sin? Why?

What does it look like both to confess and to turn away from your sins? Which is harder? In other words, is it harder to admit the sins or to make the changes necessary in light of them?

Shortly after Jesus was resurrected and ascended into heaven, the disciples preached the truth about Him in a bold, public way. Peter spoke this to a crowd in Jerusalem:

> Repent therefore, and turn back, that your sins may be blotted
> out, that times of refreshing may come from the presence of the
> Lord, and that he may send the Christ appointed for you, Jesus.
>
> **ACTS 3:19-20**

What stands out to you about these verses?

What do you think it means that "times of refreshing" (v. 19) will come after repentance and forgiveness? How does this idea affect your view of repentance?

After we confess our sin, we abandon our sin by turning away from it. We walk the other way with the help of the Holy Spirit. We receive divine empowerment to walk beyond the realm of our sin, and that's called faith.

FAITH

The most famous passage in the Bible on faith is the so-called hall of faith in Hebrews 11. That passage contains a working definition of *faith,* as well as a list of biblical heroes who lived their lives by faith. The chapter begins like this:

> ¹Faith is the assurance of things hoped for, the conviction of things not seen. ²For by it the people of old received their commendation. ³By faith we understand that the universe was created by the word of God, so that what is seen was not made out of things that are visible.
>
> **HEBREWS 11:1-3**

What does the definition of *faith* in verse 1 tell you? How is it different from or similar to your previous idea of what faith is?

What does faith allow us to do (see v. 3)?

Read this portion of the hall of faith and answer the questions that follow.

> ⁴By faith Abel offered to God a more acceptable sacrifice than Cain, through which he was commended as righteous, God commending him by accepting his gifts. And through his faith, though he died, he still speaks. ⁵By faith Enoch was taken up so that he should not see death, and he was not found, because God had taken him. Now before he was taken he was commended as having pleased God. ⁶And without faith it is impossible to please him, for whoever would draw near to God must believe that he exists and that he rewards those who seek him.

⁷By faith Noah, being warned by God concerning events as yet unseen, in reverent fear constructed an ark for the saving of his household. By this he condemned the world and became an heir of the righteousness that comes by faith. ⁸By faith Abraham obeyed when he was called to go out to a place that he was to receive as an inheritance. And he went out, not knowing where he was going. ⁹By faith he went to live in the land of promise, as in a foreign land, living in tents with Isaac and Jacob, heirs with him of the same promise. ¹⁰For he was looking forward to the city that has foundations, whose designer and builder is God. ¹¹By faith Sarah herself received power to conceive, even when she was past the age, since she considered him faithful who had promised. ¹²Therefore from one man, and him as good as dead, were born descendants as many as the stars of heaven and as many as the innumerable grains of sand by the seashore. ¹³These all died in faith, not having received the things promised, but having seen them and greeted them from afar, and having acknowledged that they were strangers and exiles on the earth.

HEBREWS 11:4-13

Go through the passage and circle the name of every person mentioned. Underline what their faith enabled them to do.

What stands out to you about these deeds of faith?

According to verse 6, our faith allows us to draw near to God and to please Him. In your life how have you drawn close to God through your faith? How do you think you've pleased God by your faith?

If you were writing yourself into the hall of faith at the end of your life, what would you want your verse to say?

By faith (insert your name and something you've done):

What do you make of verse 13, and how does it set your expectations of faith?

Our ability to grow closer to God—to be conformed to the image of Christ—depends on our ability to confess our sins, turn from our sins, and rely on God in faith to drive our efforts to repent of sin in our lives. The Holy Spirit sanctifies us, and repentance is one of the critical processes He uses to change us. We shouldn't fear it or resist it. We should wholeheartedly embrace it, as so many heroes of the faith have done.

What is the Holy Spirit's role in repentance? Spend a few moments recording your thoughts.

Finish this section by praying this prayer:

God, I thank You for living in me. I thank You for sending Your Son, Jesus Christ, to die for me and for sending your Holy Spirit to continually draw me closer to You through the gospel. I pray that You'll enable me to submit to Your sanctifying work of repentance. I ask that You'll make me aware of areas of my life that require repentance. Help me confess those sins and follow through afterward by decisively turning from those sins by the power of Your Spirit. Help me, Father, to walk by faith in Christ and to trust, as the heroes of the faith did, that You're the author of my salvation and the One who guides me through the process of repentance. Help me not to run from that process but to embrace it. Refine me through repentance, Lord, so that I can grow to be holy like Jesus. I trust You, and I love You. Amen.

We receive divine empowerment to walk beyond the realm of our sin, and that's called faith.
#UNLEASHED

GOSPEL APPLICATION

To begin our final lesson on faith and repentance, let's read a quotation by Charles Spurgeon, the lion of London, the prince of preachers. He said this on the topic of repentance:

> I learn from the Scriptures that repentance is just as necessary to salvation as faith is, and the faith that has not repentance going with it will have to be repented of. Repentance is as much a mark of a Christian, as faith is. A very little sin, as the world calls it, is a very great sin to a true Christian.[1]

As you consider what you've learned about faith and repentance this week, what do you make of this Spurgeon quotation? How does it challenge you?

How can Spurgeon's words affect the way you live out the gospel in your life?

In the New Testament repentance is primarily expressed by Greek words that mean *to understand something differently after thinking it over*. This change of mind necessarily leads to changed actions, in keeping with the Greek view that the mind controls the body. Repentance is an action. It's something we do, not something we think. True repentance leads to a changed mind and changed actions.

To bring that change about, we have to do the things we've already discussed: confess our sins, turn from our sins, and rely on our faith in God for true repentance.

Consider this passage:

> If we say we have fellowship with him while we walk in darkness, we lie and do not practice the truth. But if we walk in the light, as he is in the light, we have fellowship with one another, and the blood of Jesus his Son cleanses us from all sin. If we say we have no sin, we deceive ourselves, and the truth is not in us. If we confess our sins, he is faithful and just to forgive us our sins and to cleanse us from all unrighteousness. If we say we have not sinned, we make him a liar, and his word is not in us.
>
> **1 JOHN 1:6-10**

Look through the passage and underline all the phrases that start with "If we ..."

Look through the passage again and circle what God will do in response to those actions.

According to this passage, what are the benefits of confession and forgiveness?

What does this passage teach you about faith? About repentance?

What picture of God do you get from this text? How would you describe Him?

What practical steps can you take to walk in the light?

GODLY GRIEF VS. WORLDLY GRIEF

In 2 Corinthians we read about a very difficult season in the relationship between Paul and the church in Corinth. The church had abandoned many principles of the gospel that Paul had taught them, and some of them were no longer respecting his leadership. Paul and the church at Corinth had been engaged in heated correspondence, and 2 Corinthians is one of Paul's letters to the church during that time. Look at what he said to them:

> Even if I made you grieve with my letter, I do not regret it—though I did regret it, for I see that that letter grieved you, though only for a while. As it is, I rejoice, not because you were grieved, but because you were grieved into repenting. For you felt a godly grief, so that you suffered no loss through us. For godly grief produces a repentance that leads to salvation without regret, whereas worldly grief produces death.
> **2 CORINTHIANS 7:8-10**

In the first verse of this passage, Paul referred to a previous letter he'd sent to the Corinthians, one that was apparently harsh enough to cause them to grieve over it.

What do you notice in this passage about repentance?

Have you ever felt the "godly grief" (v. 9) Paul talked about? What did it drive you to do?

In what way is repentance the natural outflow of godly grief? Have you experienced that in your life?

Have you ever experienced worldly grief without repentance? What was that like, and how did it affect you?

How does the experience of godly grief lead you to a greater understanding and application of the gospel in your life?

THE HOLY SPIRIT EMPOWERS REPENTANCE

In 1 Corinthians Paul said the Holy Spirit enables us to call Christ our Lord:

> I want you to understand that no one speaking in the
> Spirit of God ever says "Jesus is accursed!" and no one
> can say "Jesus is Lord" except in the Holy Spirit.
> **I CORINTHIANS 12:3**

Calling Jesus Lord doesn't simply apply to our initial justification. It also applies to our sanctification. We're unable to call Jesus the Lord of our lives without the power of the Spirit. We're unable to identify our sin with the Holy Spirit's conviction. We're unable to turn from that sin in our own power. It's the Holy Spirit who enables us to truly repent and return Christ to His rightful place of lordship over our lives.

How does confession affirm the lordship of Christ in your life?

How do you think God uses repentance to further conform us to Christ's image?

Why is it important to rely on the Holy Spirit in the process of repentance? What's the alternative?

We rely on God to help us leave our sins behind, and that requires faith in Him and His work through the Holy Spirit. Removing faith from the equation of our spiritual growth in Jesus is anti-Christian in the strongest sense of the term.

PRACTICING REPENTANCE

As you've completed this week's study of faith and repentance, a number of areas in your life may have come to mind that require repentance. Some of those areas are probably obvious. Others may not seem significant, but for some reason they keep coming to your mind. Realize that God has already searched our hearts and knows our sin. He prompts us to do the same.

Let's close this session with a very practical exercise designed to propel you toward genuine repentance in your life.

First make a list of all the things you know you need to repent of.

Now circle the things on this list that you've confessed, first and foremost to God but also to any individuals who needed to hear your confession.

Finally, ask the Holy Spirit through faith to bring you to a place of genuine repentance in these areas. Begin that process by praying this prayer:

Holy Spirit, You know the sins on this list. You knew them when they were desires in my heart before I even thought them or carried them out. I confess that I [say aloud the things on your list]. I'm sorry, Lord. I genuinely grieve that I've allowed these sinful behaviors and attitudes to creep into my life. I ask You, Holy Spirit, by Your power, to remove these sins from my life. Help me move forward and grow closer to You every day. Amen.

Now make a list of things that keep coming to your mind, but for some reason you continue to doubt whether you really need to confess them or repent. Maybe you find yourself explaining them away. Even if you resist calling them sins, record them. Be honest with yourself.

Pray the following prayer and truly ask God to work in your life in these areas.

God, You know the things on this list. You know whether they're sins. You know whether I need to confess them and repent. Lord, help me see these things as You see them. Reveal to me the way I should view them. If I'm blinded by my own pride or rationalizations in these areas, remove that fog and let me see myself and these behaviors for what they really are. I want to grow closer to You, Lord. By Your Holy Spirit I want to leave anything behind that You want me to abandon. Lord, give me a repentant heart in these areas. Don't let me forget about them, but bring them to my mind and my heart if I need to deal with them and repent. I love You, Lord, and I trust You. Amen.

We never graduate from our need for true repentance. Repentance is a continuing part of our journey with God. Owning, repenting, and confessing our sin are essential steps in our lifelong process of sanctification. God lavishes us with His resources and His presence to help us pursue holiness and become conformed to the image of the Lord Jesus Christ. By faith and through repentance, God unleashes His power in our lives.

Finish this section of study by praying this prayer:

Holy Spirit, I'm so thankful that You're living inside me and that You know me better than I know myself. I'm thankful that You love me more than I could ever imagine and that You know what's best for me. I acknowledge that I'm a sinful person. I acknowledge that in order to be conformed to the image of Christ, I need to confess my sins and turn away from them. I have faith that this is something You're able to do through Your Holy Spirit. I acknowledge that I can never truly repent in my own strength. Help me see the areas of my life where I need to grow. Give me humility to pursue repentance so that I can grow spiritually and look more and more like Jesus. I submit myself to You and Your will. I love You, Lord, and I ask that You'll refine me through repentance. Amen.

1. Charles Spurgeon, *Christ Alone* [online, cited 4 December 2015]. Available from the Internet: *www.Christalone.com.*

By faith and through repentance,
God unleashes His power in our lives.
#UNLEASHED

THE ROLE OF SUFFERING IN SANCTIFICATION

START

Welcome to session 3 of *Unleashed*. Open the group session by asking participants to discuss the following questions.

As you completed this week's personal study, what did the Lord show you? How did He speak to you?

What role do you believe suffering plays in spiritual growth?

Have you experienced doubt or anger toward God because of suffering (in your life or someone else's)?

Suffering is a common obstacle to faith. People who don't know God can have difficulty reconciling suffering with the idea of a God who loves us. Suffering is also a primary catalyst for doubt among believers because we tend to feel that if we're faithful to God, He should be faithful to us and shelter us from suffering. We're tempted to think God doesn't love us or is punishing us if we go through a season of suffering. The pain of our trial clouds our ability to see God clearly, making it difficult for us to comprehend the possibility that He might have a purpose for our pain.

Today we'll hear Pastor Mason talk about the role of suffering in our spiritual lives. We'll see that suffering plays a critical role in our sanctification, especially if we're willing to trust God through the process and submit to His refining work.

Watch video session 3, in which Pastor Mason examines the difficult subject of suffering and provides biblical truth about the way God can use it to conform us to the image of His Son.

WATCH

The thief comes only to steal and kill and destroy.
I came that they may have life and have it abundantly.
JOHN 10:10

From that time Jesus began to show his disciples that he must
go to Jerusalem and suffer many things from the elders and chief
priests and scribes, and be killed, and on the third day be raised.
MATTHEW 16:21

Since we have been justified by faith, we have peace with God through our
Lord Jesus Christ. Through him we have also obtained access by faith into this
grace in which we stand, and we rejoice in hope of the glory of God. More
than that, but we rejoice in our sufferings, knowing that suffering produces
endurance, and endurance produces character, and character produces
hope, and hope does not put us to shame, because God's love has been
poured into our hearts through the Holy Spirit who has been given to us.
ROMANS 5:1-5

Count it all joy, my brothers, when you meet trials of various kinds, for
you know that the testing of your faith produces steadfastness. And let
steadfastness have its full effect, that you may be perfect and complete,
lacking in nothing. If any of you lacks wisdom, let him ask God, who
gives generously to all without reproach, and it will be given him.
JAMES 1:2-5

We are afflicted in every way, but not crushed; perplexed, but not driven
to despair; persecuted, but not forsaken; struck down, but not destroyed.
2 CORINTHIANS 4:8-9

I consider that the sufferings of this present time are not worth
comparing with the glory that is to be revealed to us.
ROMANS 8:18

Beloved, do not be surprised at the fiery trial when it comes upon
you to test you, as though something strange were happening
to you. But rejoice insofar as you share Christ's sufferings, that
you may also rejoice and be glad when his glory is revealed.
I PETER 4:12-13

RESPOND

Pastor Mason covered a very difficult subject in this session, one that often leads people either to a new depth of faith or to a season of distance from God.

> What stood out to you most in this session?

> Have you experienced a season of suffering? If so, how did it affect your relationship with God or your understanding of who He is?

Many of us struggle to understand why God allows suffering in our lives.

> What do you think about the fact that many of the early Christian leaders, including most of Jesus' disciples, suffered for their faith?

> How can suffering be a means of God's grace, as Pastor Mason said?

> What do you think about the sculptor analogy from the video? How might God use suffering to chisel you into the image of Christ?

> What did you find the most surprising about Pastor Mason's message in this video?

In closing, pray and thank God for allowing us to grow closer to Him through all circumstances, even in the midst of our suffering. Also thank Him for sending His Son to suffer on our behalf.

Complete the following three personal-study sections before the next group session. One section will focus on this week's big idea, the next section will dig deeper into Scripture, and the final section will focus on application.

THE BIG IDEA

Growing up in D.C. during the late 1970s and early '80s was as fun as it was dangerous. It was fun because in this city we learned to become innovative by creating for ourselves what wasn't available otherwise. Everything that might have been readily available to other communities had to be invented with what we had available in ours. We had a lot of fun doing that.

But our context was dangerous too. The sound of gunshots became the background noise to all the fun we had as kids. Friends were being killed or incarcerated. I wanted out! My quest became leaving, never to return to this type of urban environment again. For me, getting out of the inner city was the natural progression of life. It represented hope that life was going to get better and the belief that I was on a positive path. My goal was to build a life that was impervious to suffering—financial suffering, dangerous neighborhoods, inadequate education, and so on. I went to college just to get out—and got hit up with the gospel. I was discipled two years later, was called to the ministry, and landed in seminary one year after that.

While at Dallas Theological Seminary, I was assigned to write a paper on sanctification. As I surveyed the New Testament and began isolating verses from Matthew to Revelation, I found that suffering is a major factor in encouraging a Christian's spiritual growth. Jesus, James, Paul, and Peter spoke about the expectation of suffering for believers. The Lord uses suffering from without and within as a means to grow us in Him and to conform us to the image of Jesus Christ.

JESUS SUFFERED

Scripture shows us that suffering played a major role even in the life of Jesus, specifically in His divinely ordained work as the Suffering Servant who was slain for the sin of all humankind. Seven centuries before Jesus was born, the prophet Isaiah vividly predicted the suffering of the Messiah:

> He was despised and rejected by men;
>   a man of sorrows, and acquainted with grief;
> and as one from whom men hide their faces
>   he was despised, and we esteemed him not.
> Surely he has borne our griefs
>   and carried our sorrows;

yet we esteemed him stricken,
    smitten by God, and afflicted.
But he was pierced for our transgressions;
    he was crushed for our iniquities;
upon him was the chastisement that brought us peace,
    and with his wounds we are healed.
All we like sheep have gone astray;
    we have turned—every one—to his own way;
and the Lord has laid on him
    the iniquity of us all.
He was oppressed, and he was afflicted,
    yet he opened not his mouth;
like a lamb that is led to the slaughter,
    and like a sheep that before its shearers is silent,
    so he opened not his mouth.
By oppression and judgment he was taken away;
    and as for his generation, who considered
that he was cut off out of the land of the living,
    stricken for the transgression of my people?
And they made his grave with the wicked
    and with a rich man in his death,
although he had done no violence,
    and there was no deceit in his mouth.
Yet it was the will of the Lord to crush him;
    he has put him to grief;
when his soul makes an offering for guilt,
    he shall see his offspring; he shall prolong his days;
the will of the Lord shall prosper in his hand.
Out of the anguish of his soul he shall see and be satisfied;
by his knowledge shall the righteous one, my servant,
    make many to be accounted righteous,
    and he shall bear their iniquities.
Therefore I will divide him a portion with the many,
    and he shall divide the spoil with the strong,
because he poured out his soul to death
    and was numbered with the transgressors;
yet he bore the sin of many,
    and makes intercession for the transgressors.

ISAIAH 53:3-12

Go back through the previous passage and underline every way Isaiah predicted the Messiah would suffer.

Now circle every reason the Messiah would suffer.

What does it mean to you to know that God had always intended for His Son to suffer?

What does this text illuminate about God? About you?

When Jesus walked the earth in the flesh, He was clearly cognizant of the fact that He would suffer. In Mark 8:31 Jesus began to teach His disciples that "the Son of Man must suffer many things and be rejected by the elders and the chief priests and the scribes and be killed, and after three days rise again." Jesus made the same prediction in Mark 9:31; 10:33-34. Jesus knew He would suffer.

How does the fact that Jesus knew He would suffer change the way you view Him?

What does Jesus' suffering teach you about your own suffering?

Suffering is antithetical to who we are because as humans, we're driven by self-preservation. We try to protect ourselves by minimizing danger where we work, where we go, and where we live. There's nothing wrong with wanting to be safe, but a Christian's drive must always originate in the gospel, not merely in self-preservation.

THE CHISELING WORK OF SUFFERING

The writer of Hebrews lets us know that Jesus, in His humanity, learned how to obey His Father through His suffering. The wording in Hebrews is poignant:

> In the days of his flesh, Jesus offered up prayers and supplications,
> with loud cries and tears, to him who was able to save him from death,
> and he was heard because of his reverence. Although he was a son, he
> learned obedience through what he suffered. And being made perfect,
> he became the source of eternal salvation to all who obey him.
>
> **HEBREWS 5:7-9**

This passage says Jesus had been "made perfect" (v. 9). That phrase is in the passive voice, pointing to the fact that Jesus didn't perfect Himself. God is the agent who acts on the recipient. Even though Jesus was born perfect in both His humanity and His divine nature, in His humanity He learned. "Learned obedience" (v. 8) means that in His humanity Jesus submitted to growth. God the Father sanctified Him. Jesus wasn't being perfected from a sin nature; He was merely maturing in His already perfected perfection.

Like us, Jesus depended on the Holy Spirit to grow, and suffering was a part of His sanctification. If Jesus, being sinless, embraced suffering in order to grow in His Father, how much more do we need to submit to God's chiseling work to carve us into the image of Christ?

Describe a time in your life when you embraced suffering. What did God show you through that experience?

Have you ever felt God working on your heart through suffering, even if you didn't embrace it? What was that experience like, and what did you learn?

As a pastor, I spend a lot of time helping Christians come to terms with difficult circumstances that God allows. When I tell people one reason they're suffering is because they're being sanctified, many want to punch my face off, and I don't blame them. It's difficult to comprehend God's graciousness to us through suffering. Peter addressed this truth in one of his letters, written to a body of believers experiencing suffering through persecution. He wrote:

> What credit is it if, when you sin and are beaten for it, you endure? But if when you do good and suffer for it you endure, this is a gracious thing in the sight of God. For to this you have been called, because Christ also suffered for you, leaving you an example, so that you might follow in his steps. He committed no sin, neither was deceit found in his mouth. When he was reviled, he did not revile in return; when he suffered, he did not threaten, but continued entrusting himself to him who judges justly.
>
> I PETER 2:20-23

What do you think Peter was saying in these verses?

How do these words challenge your faith in God?

As a pastor, I'm always deeply empathetic about the suffering of Christians I know, but I'm also hopeful for their endurance. If God is doing a good work in my people, I don't want it to stop until God is finished blessing them, difficult though it is to bear. I want the power of God to be unleashed in their lives.

A CASE STUDY FROM JOB

In the midst of our suffering, we're constantly tempted to think, *God doesn't care* or *God isn't good.* We're all tempted to ask the question "If God is all-powerful, why does He allow me to go through this?" One of the most telling statements on this topic in Scripture is the voice of Job. After great calamity in Job's life, his wife said to him, "Do you still hold fast your integrity? Curse God and die" (Job 2:9).

Job's wife couldn't fathom God's activity in the midst of hardship. Her statement is a warning to all of us who follow Christ. If we're to persevere in the midst of pain, we must possess a deep conviction of the unmoving character of God that's embedded in the depths of our heart soil and an understanding of God's sanctifying work in the midst of our pain. Job had that deep conviction, as demonstrated by his response to his wife:

> "You speak as one of the foolish women would speak.
> Shall we receive good from God, and shall we not receive
> evil?" In all this Job did not sin with his lips.
> **JOB 2:10**

What does it take to have and maintain a deep conviction of God's unmoving character—the kind Job had?

Why do you think it's so difficult to maintain a right view of God when we're suffering?

When you're going through something difficult, how does God look to you?
What caricature of Him are you tempted to see?

Suffering can be used to chisel us into the image of Christ, but Satan will use it to spread lies about the character of God and about His promises to us. Job remembered the promises of God in the worst of circumstances, and his example is a lesson for all of us. We mustn't let suffering choke out of us the truth about who God is. Suffering reveals who's anchoring us at all times. Are our lives anchored in our circumstances or in the God of the ages?

In our journey with Christ under the sovereign, omniscient sight of the good Lord, both good and evil will cross our paths. And during both the Lord remains the same.

Finish this section of study by praying this prayer:

Dear Lord, I thank You for loving me. You love me so much that You sent Your Son to suffer and die for me. You planned to send Him to suffer long before He ever arrived on this earth in the flesh. Lord Jesus, You knew You'd be crucified at the end of your earthly ministry, and yet You willingly went to the cross on my behalf. Thank You, Lord! May I never lose sight of that deliberate sacrifice. Lord, when I'm suffering, help me remember that You've suffered for me, that I'm in a sense following in Your footsteps. Help me retain a clear picture of who You really are and grow through the experience in all the ways You want me to. I love You, Lord, and I trust You. Amen.

The Lord uses suffering from without and within as a means to grow us in Him and to conform us to the image of Jesus Christ.
#UNLEASHED

DIGGING DEEPER

This week we're studying the role of suffering in our sanctification. We've seen that God always intended for His Messiah to suffer (see Isa. 53), that Jesus knew He'd suffer (see Mark 8–10), that God used this suffering in Jesus' life (see Heb. 5), and that our circumstances shouldn't dictate our view of God (see the Book of Job). Now let's explore the critical question "What causes our suffering?" There are three primary causes: our fallen world, sinful lifestyles, and spiritual warfare.

THE FALLEN WORLD

If you live in this world, believer or not, you'll experience the tragic results of Papa Adam's sin. In the Book of Genesis, God created Adam and Eve to live in the garden of Eden in God's presence, a place without pain, sin, or death. God warned them that pain and death would result if they ate from the tree of the knowledge of good and evil or even if they touched it. Duped by Satan, Adam and Eve ate from the tree. This event is known as the fall. After Adam and Eve sinned and ate the fruit, God articulated the consequences:

> To the woman he said,
> "I will surely multiply your pain in childbearing;
>   in pain you shall bring forth children.
> Your desire shall be for your husband,
>   and he shall rule over you."
> And to Adam he said,
> "Because you have listened to the voice of your wife
>   and have eaten of the tree
> of which I commanded you,
>   'You shall not eat of it,'
> cursed is the ground because of you;
>   in pain you shall eat of it all the days of your life;
> thorns and thistles it shall bring forth for you;
>   and you shall eat the plants of the field.
> By the sweat of your face
>   you shall eat bread,
> till you return to the ground,
>   for out of it you were taken;
> for you are dust,
>   and to dust you shall return."

The man called his wife's name Eve, because she was the mother of all living. And the LORD God made for Adam and for his wife garments of skins and clothed them. Then the LORD God said, "Behold, the man has become like one of us in knowing good and evil. Now, lest he reach out his hand and take also of the tree of life and eat, and live forever—" therefore the LORD God sent him out from the garden of Eden to work the ground from which he was taken. He drove out the man, and at the east of the garden of Eden he placed the cherubim and a flaming sword that turned every way to guard the way to the tree of life.

GENESIS 3:16-24

Underline every consequence of the fall listed in this passage.

What do you notice about the consequences? What would be the long-term repercussions of Adam and Eve's decision?

Adam's sin brought about cataclysmic consequences for all humanity, who would subsequently be born sinful. In Psalm 51 David asked for God's mercy and forgiveness after committing serious sins. In that psalm he mentioned the fact that we're born into sin:

Wash me thoroughly from my iniquity,
    and cleanse me from my sin!
For I know my transgressions,
    and my sin is ever before me.
Against you, you only, have I sinned
    and done what is evil in your sight,
so that you may be justified in your words
    and blameless in your judgment.
Behold, I was brought forth in iniquity,
    and in sin did my mother conceive me.

PSALM 51:2-5

Paul also drew a contrast between Adam's actions and Christ's actions. Adam's sin had lasting consequences for all of us, but Christ's actions will undo all that:

As one trespass led to condemnation for all men, so one act
of righteousness leads to justification and life for all men. For
as by the one man's disobedience the many were made sinners,
so by the one man's obedience the many will be made righteous.

ROMANS 5:18-19

What kinds of emotions are evoked when you read the passages from Psalms and Romans?

According to the Romans passage, what were the long-term consequences of Adam's actions?

We all live in the consequences of the fall. We can no longer live in God's perfect presence as Adam and Eve did in the garden of Eden before the fall. We're born sinful into a broken world. The fall also brought about the universal brokenness of our world, now groaning over its condition through natural disasters and decay. In Romans 8 Paul pointed out that the world itself is fallen, not just the people who inhabit it:

> The creation was subjected to futility, not willingly, but because of him who subjected it, in hope that the creation itself will be set free from its bondage to corruption and obtain the freedom of the glory of the children of God. For we know that the whole creation has been groaning together in the pains of childbirth until now. And not only the creation, but we ourselves, who have the firstfruits of the Spirit, groan inwardly as we wait eagerly for adoption as sons, the redemption of our bodies.
> **ROMANS 8:20-23**

How does this passage describe the extent to which brokenness and suffering exist? What does this mean for us today?

Underline every occurrence of the word *creation*. What was Paul saying about the created world?

Identify evidence that you've been born into sin or that creation is groaning.

All suffering finds its root, on some level, in the fall. No matter what type of person someone is morally or religiously, he or she is affected by the fall. But with confidence we can know that in the middle of suffering created by sin, God has initiated a plan of deliverance for His people and all creation from the subjugation of sin.

We can and must seek to experience Christlike growth in the middle of our suffering. This happens when we're reminded of and respond to the freedom we have over sin that comes from the suffering and death of Christ on our behalf.

SINFUL LIFESTYLES AND SYSTEMS: THE FLESH

Suffering also occurs as a consequence of our personal sin and systems of sin that result from our fallen nature. Because of our natural tendency to sin, given to us from Adam, we suffer under the tyranny of the flesh. Personal sins like greed, pride, and sexual immorality can cause personal suffering. So in addition to the fallen state of our world because of Adam, our own sinful choices can bring suffering into our experience.

For instance, if we have a child out of wedlock, we can find ourselves paying child support, which could become a burden to our finances and cause economic suffering. God can redeem the situation, but sometimes He doesn't remove all the consequences. For a believer, these consequences should be seen as the discipline of the Lord. Yet God can use even our most difficult suffering to mold us into the image of Christ. Consider this text from Hebrews:

> "The Lord disciplines the one he loves,
>   and chastises every son whom he receives."
> It is for discipline that you have to endure. God is treating you as sons.
> For what son is there whom his father does not discipline? If you are
> left without discipline, in which all have participated, then you are
> illegitimate children and not sons. Besides this, we have had earthly
> fathers who disciplined us and we respected them. Shall we not much
> more be subject to the Father of spirits and live? For they disciplined
> us for a short time as it seemed best to them, but he disciplines us
> for our good, that we may share his holiness. For the moment all
> discipline seems painful rather than pleasant, but later it yields the
> peaceful fruit of righteousness to those who have been trained by it.
>
> **HEBREWS 12:6-11**

Circle every form of the word *discipline* in this passage. Make a note beside each use of the word to indicate the point the author was making.

Record a one-sentence summary of the author's point about discipline.

Individual sin, however, isn't the only form of suffering we endure. No person is an island to himself, and corporate sin creates systemic problems in our society. Sin works like a virus in our communities; one person's sinful disposition can infect his neighbor's. This is why Paul so aggressively condemned false teachers and others who led people into sin. Systemic sin is contagious like a pathogen, eating away at individuals' consciences.

Social policies can be made to preserve and promote sin. Just think of the Jim Crow laws, or Hitler's Aryan clause. Millions of people suffered, not just individually but as an entire nation. Everything from racism to socioeconomic oppression can become a system of sin that causes suffering. But even then, even when all the odds are stacked against us, God can use that oppression to sanctify us.

What systems of sin have you observed in your nation or community?

In what systems of sin have you participated? How have you repented of these and confessed them to the Lord?

SPIRITUAL WARFARE: THE DEVIL

The Bible says our war isn't against flesh and blood but against an invisible Enemy who wreaks havoc on couples, singles, families, sons, and daughters. Satan, the great deceiver, works in the inner city as well as the suburbs. He lays siege to both bedrooms and board-rooms. The great liar who tempted Eve in the garden, as well as Jesus in the desert, doesn't discriminate. He's an equal-opportunity destroyer.

Sometimes when we suffer, it's nothing less than an attack from the serpent. Though spiritual warfare is related to both the fall and the flesh, suffering at the hands of Satan is a unique type of suffering. In these times of suffering, God has given us clear instructions to engage in battle as warriors who put on the whole armor of God:

> Put on the whole armor of God, that you may be able to stand against
> the schemes of the devil. For we do not wrestle against flesh and blood,
> but against the rulers, against the authorities, against the cosmic
> powers over this present darkness, against the spiritual forces of evil

in the heavenly places. Therefore take up the whole armor of God, that you may be able to withstand in the evil day, and having done all, to stand firm. Stand therefore, having fastened on the belt of truth, and having put on the breastplate of righteousness, and, as shoes for your feet, having put on the readiness given by the gospel of peace. In all circumstances take up the shield of faith, with which you can extinguish all the flaming darts of the evil one; and take the helmet of salvation, and the sword of the Spirit, which is the word of God.

EPHESIANS 6:11-17

Think of the suffering you're currently experiencing and have experienced in the past. How can the armor described in Paul's letter provide protection against the Enemy's attacks?

What's the one piece of armor you most often fail to put on? What steps can you take to reverse this neglect?

Finish this section of study by praying that the Lord will teach you to turn to Him when you suffer, cry out to Him, and yield to His sanctifying work to conform you to the likeness of Jesus.

God can use even our most difficult suffering to mold us into the image of Christ.
#UNLEASHED

GOSPEL APPLICATION

In the previous lesson we saw that there are several causes of suffering, some outside our control (the fall and Satan's schemes) and some within our control (our own sinful choices). Regardless of how the suffering occurs, it can be a painful season we often want to escape, and it tests our faithfulness to God. But the good news is that Christian faithfulness is an act of God, not something we can attain through moralistic acts of our own volition. God makes Christians worthy through the gospel.

Have you ever thought about your faithfulness being given to you by God instead of acquiring it through your own power? How have you been aligning or maybe misaligning your life with this truth?

In my sermon preparation I get a lot of opportunities to wrestle with the Lord and His Word. I wrestle with the implications, application, and transformation of the gospel. The reason I call it wrestling is that if I'm honest, I don't like everything in God's Word. However, my like or dislike of what God says doesn't make truth truth, but Jesus does. Therefore, I recognize my need to come into alignment with what the Lord says.

What kinds of suffering are you currently experiencing?

In what way(s) do you need to align with the Lord in these areas of suffering?

In 2 Thessalonians Paul was writing to a congregation that was experiencing deep levels of suffering. In the midst of all the suffering they were going through, Paul, being a good shepherd, sought to ground their understanding in the gospel. He wrote, "To this end we always pray for you, that our God may make you worthy of his calling" (2 Thess. 1:11).

We need to recognize the nature of Paul's prayer. He didn't pray a triumphant prayer of deliverance but something totally different. In a very real sense, he prayed for God to keep them in their trial. Some people would rebuke such a prayer in our entitled culture.

Is it wrong to pray for deliverance? No. However, Paul understood that every hardship we face is an opportunity for God to shape and transform us.

> **How do you feel about the idea that God would keep us in a trial to make us more like Jesus?**

We see the same principle at work in a passage from Daniel. Three of Daniel's friends—Shadrach, Meshach, and Abednego—were being threatened by the Babylonian king, Nebuchadnezzar, because they refused to worship an idol he'd built. When he threatened to throw them into a fiery furnace as punishment, they said this in response:

> [16]Shadrach, Meshach, and Abednego answered and said to the king,
> "O Nebuchadnezzar, we have no need to answer you in this matter.
> [17]If this be so, our God whom we serve is able to deliver us from the
> burning fiery furnace, and he will deliver us out of your hand,
> O king. [18]But if not, be it known to you, O king, that we will not
> serve your gods or worship the golden image that you have set up."
> **DANIEL 3:16-18**

> **Underline the words "But if not" at the beginning of verse 18. What's the significance of these words?**

> **What does the men's response teach you about faith in the midst of suffering?**

> **In what way is their response countercultural?**

Also consider David's praise of the way God had dealt with him in times of struggle:

> Answer me when I call, O God of my righteousness!
> You have given me relief when I was in distress.
> **PSALM 4:1**

Relief here means *to have a momentary or sustained alleviation of trouble or anxiety*. God can keep you in a trial but give you a sense of deliverance within the trial without completely removing it. What a powerful prayer David composed! "Lord, under the pressure of the circumstances, even if You don't deliver me, make room for me to feel delivered even if I'm not." On the surface it may seem to be a faithless prayer, but on the contrary, it's a prayer of deep faith.

> Have you ever experienced a divine sense of deliverance within a great trial? How did it make you feel?

> What would it take for you to respond as David did in the previous psalm?

Paul's prayer was similar for the Thessalonians: "God, don't deliver them; use them while they're in their trial." Many psalms speak of God delivering. There's nothing wrong with a prayer for deliverance, but Paul emphasized the Christians' growth above that of any temporal goal.

THE WHY OF SUFFERING

Fifteen years ago my wife and I experienced our first pregnancy, a girl. We were in our last semester of seminary, and we were excited about graduation and a new church. February 5, 2000, I had an Old Testament class that I really needed to attend, but Yvette had a doctor's appointment scheduled at the same time. We both agreed that because the pregnancy was going so well, it wouldn't hurt anything for me to miss her appointment.

While in class, I received a series of frantic calls from Yvette to call and come to the hospital. I left class and learned that at six months of pregnancy, the baby had no heartbeat. When I got to the hospital, my wife and I wept bitterly. The doctor reinitiated the sonogram, but there was still no breath or heartbeat. Several times we prayed and entreated the Lord for a favorable response, but heaven seemed to be silent.

Naomi's death was the first real test of my faith and our faith as a couple. What were we to think of God? Why did He allow people who were serving Him to experience something so catastrophic?

Why is the question many of us ask of the Lord when something tragic happens in our lives or in the life of someone we know. There's story after story of suffering in the Bible, but very seldom do we know why the people suffered. On this topic Paul wrote:

> We rejoice in our sufferings, knowing that suffering produces endurance, and endurance produces character, and character produces hope, and hope does not put us to shame, because God's love has been poured into our hearts through the Holy Spirit who has been given to us.
> **ROMANS 5:3-5**

Rejoicing in the midst of suffering focuses our attention on the knowledge of what the Spirit produces in us through that suffering. The result is threefold: suffering produces endurance, endurance produces character, and character produces hope.

Have you ever experienced rejoicing in the midst of suffering? What was that like, and what did you learn from it?

SUFFERING UNLEASHES ENDURANCE

A while back I began going to a gym regularly, and for the first time in my life, I stuck to the treadmill. After some time disciplining myself to the regimen, it became easier to me, and I had to increase the challenge to continue growing in endurance.

Suffering is the believer's being thrown onto the treadmill of life's challenges. Endurance in the Bible is similar; it means steadfast adherence to a course of action in spite of difficulties and testing. As we go through trials, we develop greater perseverance to deal with increased challenges. Consider James's words on the subject:

> Count it all joy, my brothers, when you meet trials of various kinds, for you know that the testing of your faith produces steadfastness. And let steadfastness have its full effect, that you may be perfect and complete, lacking in nothing. If any of you lacks wisdom, let him ask God, who gives generously to all without reproach, and it will be given him.
> **JAMES 1:2-5**

How does this passage compare with Romans 5:3-5?

What would it look like to embrace this mentality during an experience of suffering? Do you think it's even possible, and if so, how?

ENDURANCE UNLEASHES CHARACTER

As God produces in us greater fortitude and capacity to deal with more hardship, He brings out character. Character is the image of Christ that's present in us being made clearer. In essence, *character* means *to expose the quality of what's being tested*.

In the heat of suffering, God gives grace for us to endure. A goldsmith uses heat under a smelting pot to bring the impurities to the top, which are skimmed off, leaving only the pure gold behind. In the same way, God uses our suffering to bring out the impurities in our lives and remove them. Peter alluded to this concept in 1 Peter 1:

> In this you rejoice, though now for a little while, if necessary,
> you have been grieved by various trials, so that the tested
> genuineness of your faith—more precious than gold that perishes
> though it is tested by fire—may be found to result in praise
> and glory and honor at the revelation of Jesus Christ.
> I PETER 1:6-7

The smelter knows the gold is ready to come off the heat when he sees his face in the melted metal. There are no impurities left to obscure his reflection. When the goldsmith sees his reflection, he knows the precious metal is now ready to be molded into what he desires. This is a picture of the way God brings out our character through suffering.

This is a tough question. If your life were molten gold and God were the goldsmith, what impurities would float to the surface—things He'd need to skim off the top in order to see His reflection in you? Be honest and thorough in your answer.

CHARACTER UNLEASHES HOPE

Character that's sanctified by the gospel becomes progressively more stable and is therefore able to focus more effectively on the things of the Lord. Character unleashes hope in suffering. Hope is the joyful expectation of what the Lord has promised. Paul wrote:

> May the God of hope fill you with all joy and peace in believing,
> so that by the power of the Holy Spirit you may abound in hope.
> **ROMANS 15:13**

How do you think your character enables you to hope in the Lord?

As disciples of Jesus, we must use hard times to harness who we really are in Christ. Until the earthen vessel is broken, the treasure within it can't be seen. Likewise, as our brokenness is exposed, Jesus is seen. It's glorious to know that a Christian's suffering in this life isn't a denial of who Christ is but an affirmation. As we experience hardship, every test of the living God finds us transformed into pure gold for His glory.

Finish this section of study by asking the Lord to help you evaluate how you're responding to your suffering. Are you using suffering as an opportunity to submit to God's sanctifying work in your life, or are you treading water until the suffering subsides? Ask God to align your understanding about the role of suffering in sanctification with the truth found in His Word.

Hope is the joyful expectation of what the Lord has promised.
#UNLEASHED

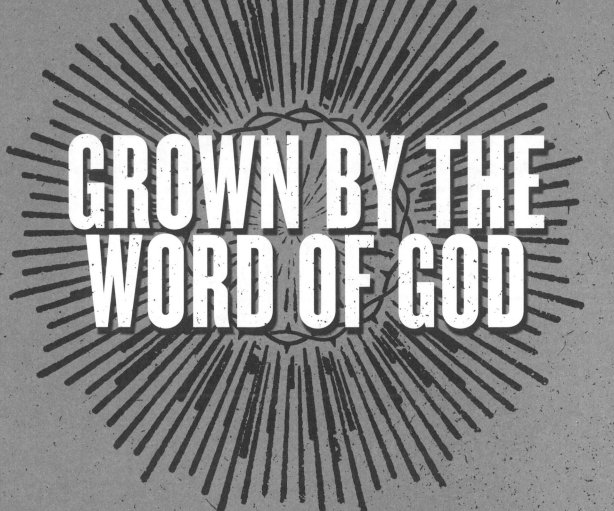

GROWN BY THE WORD OF GOD

START

Welcome to session 4 of *Unleashed*. Open the group session by asking participants to discuss the following questions.

> As you completed this week's personal study, what did the Lord show you?
> How did He speak to you?

> If someone asked you why reading the Bible is important, what would you say?

> Why do you think it's a challenge for many of us to read the Bible consistently?

Bible reading is on the decline today. This phenomenon has been observed by pastors, Christian college professors, and research organizations that study trends in the church. In previous generations most Christians were equipped with a basic level of biblical knowledge. A general familiarity with Scripture came with faith in Christ—a knowledge passed on by parents to their children, as well as through the church. This general familiarity with the Bible is no longer commonplace. Regardless of the reasons for this decline in biblical engagement, the importance of regularly reading Scripture remains as crucial as ever for those of us who follow Christ.

Today we'll hear Pastor Mason talk about the importance of reading God's Word to further our sanctification. It's the foundational spiritual discipline from which all others derive, and its importance can't be overstated.

Watch video session 4, in which Pastor Mason helps us understand the significance of God's Word for our spiritual growth.

WATCH

The word of God is living and active, sharper than any two-edged sword, piercing to the division of soul and of spirit, of joints and of marrow, and discerning the thoughts and intentions of the heart.

HEBREWS 4:12

Sanctify them in the truth; your word is truth.

JOHN 17:17

Put away all filthiness and rampant wickedness and receive with meekness the implanted word, which is able to save your souls.

JAMES 1:21

When anyone hears the word of the kingdom and does not understand it, the evil one comes and snatches away what has been sown in his heart. This is what was sown along the path. As for what was sown on rocky ground, this is the one who hears the word and immediately receives it with joy, yet he has no root in himself, but endures for a while, and when tribulation or persecution arises on account of the word, immediately he falls away. As for what was sown among thorns, this is the one who hears the word, but the cares of the world and the deceitfulness of riches choke the word, and it proves unfruitful. As for what was sown on good soil, this is the one who hears the word and understands it. He indeed bears fruit and yields, in one case a hundredfold, in another sixty, and in another thirty.

MATTHEW 13:19-23

The Helper, the Holy Spirit, whom the Father will send in my name, he will teach you all things and bring to your remembrance all that I have said to you.

JOHN 14:26

RESPOND

As Pastor Mason explained in this session, the Word of God is the main ingredient in our spiritual growth, illuminating God's will and making us aware of all the other means God uses to sanctify us.

> **What stood out to you most in this session?**

> **Do you find it difficult to consistently read the Bible? What's the biggest obstacle for you?**

Psalm 1 encourages us to delight in God's Word—to meditate on it day and night.

> **Have you ever experienced delight in God's Word? If so, what were the circumstances that produced the feeling, and how can you repeat that experience?**

> **What would it look like for you to meditate on God's Word day and night?**

Pastor Mason listed four different ways to engage with the Bible: hearing it, reading it, studying it, and meditating on it.

> **Which of these four do you struggle with? Which come to you most naturally? What steps can you take to incorporate all four elements into your life?**

> **What did you find most inspiring about Pastor Mason's teaching in this session? How do you plan to take the next step?**

In closing, pray and thank God for choosing to make Himself known to us through His Word. Also ask Him to show you how to take in more of His Word each day.

Complete the following three personal-study sections before the next group session. One section will focus on this week's big idea, the next section will dig deeper into Scripture, and the final section will focus on application.

THE BIG IDEA

I love to watch "Chopped," a show on the Food Network that features world-class chefs who are given mystery ingredients to compete in preparing a three-course meal. Many times the ingredients are exotic items that aren't easily mixed into the same dishes. Chefs are judged on their ability to highlight the ingredients in a way that displays great presentation, taste, and creativity. In most episodes at least one chef forgets to add the key ingredient or fails to properly feature the key ingredient. This chef usually loses the competition.

The Word of God is like that. It's an essential ingredient in our sanctification and growth. The Holy Spirit sanctifies us through God's Word. In fact, it's impossible to grow in Christ without the Word of God. The Word of God is a gateway to the means of grace. What I mean by *gateway* is that all the ways we grow in Christ are contained in Scripture. We wouldn't know God, Jesus, the gospel, or any means necessary for spiritual growth without the Word of God.

This week we'll delve into the role of the Word of God in unleashing the sanctifying work of the Holy Spirit. We'll look at basic ways we can interact practically with God's Word.

Here are a few classic texts on the importance of God's Word in our lives. Read each one and honestly answer the questions that follow.

Do your best to present yourself to God as one approved, a worker who has no need to be ashamed, rightly handling the word of truth.
2 TIMOTHY 2:15

According to this verse, what does it mean to be approved?

What does it look like for you to rightly handle the word of truth?

If you gave yourself a grade on how well you handle God's Word, what would that grade be and why?

God watches our lives now, but there will definitely be a moment in the future when we'll have to give an account for the way we lived our lives (see Rom. 14:10; 2 Cor. 5:10).

How does the knowledge that you'll "present yourself to God" (2 Tim. 2:15) affect your faith?

Is this fact motivating or discouraging? Why or why not?

All Scripture is breathed out by God and profitable for teaching,
for reproof, for correction, and for training in righteousness, that
the man of God may be competent, equipped for every good work.
2 TIMOTHY 3:16-17

Of the four uses of Scripture outlined in these verses, which do you have the most experience with? Which do you struggle with?

What's the purpose of Scripture, according to these verses?

What does it mean to you to know that *all* Scripture is from God? Are there parts of the Bible you gravitate toward or parts you haven't valued highly enough?

"All Scripture" (v. 16) means every book, every paragraph, and every verse in the revealed Word of God. The more I do expositional preaching through particular books of the Bible, the more I recognize that God doesn't waste His breath. From the popular books and verses to the so-called minor and obscure, all of God's Word matters for our sanctification—for God's process of conforming us to the image of Jesus. Peter wrote:

> [19] We have the prophetic word more fully confirmed, to which you will do well to pay attention as to a lamp shining in a dark place, until the day dawns and the morning star rises in your hearts, [20] knowing this first of all, that no prophecy of Scripture comes from someone's own interpretation. [21] For no prophecy was ever produced by the will of man, but men spoke from God as they were carried along by the Holy Spirit.
>
> **2 PETER 1:19-21**

How do these verses compare with Paul's words in 2 Timothy 3:16-17? What similarities do you notice?

What does it mean to pay attention to the Word as if it's "a lamp shining in a dark place" (2 Pet. 1:19)?

What's the significance of verses 20-21? What does this mean for your personal study of Scripture?

The breathing out of God's Word is a magnificent truth. Although God recorded His Word through human authors, He's the One who initiated it, thereby making the Bible His Word. To put it succinctly, God is the divine Author of the Bible.

Unlike human beings, who can utter thousands on thousands of words to no effect, when God speaks, things happen. The connection between the Word of God and creation is not the only exhibition of God's power. Rather, God's word that brought the universe into existence is the same means by which He saves people from sin and death. The same breath that infused life into Adam's lungs was the same breath that uttered the words of life in the Sermon on the Mount. Amazing, humbling, and mind-blowing.

Have you thought of Jesus as the Author of the whole Bible? Why or why not?

How does the idea that Jesus authored the Old Testament change the way you view Him?

Toward the end of His earthly ministry, Jesus prayed a very powerful prayer for His disciples. On the eve of his arrest, trial, and crucifixion, He prayed these powerful words to our Heavenly Father:

> [14]I have given them your word, and the world has hated them because they are not of the world, just as I am not of the world. [15]I do not ask that you take them out of the world, but that you keep them from the evil one. [16]They are not of the world, just as I am not of the world. [17]Sanctify them in the truth; your word is truth. [18]As you sent me into the world, so I have sent them into the world. [19]And for their sake I consecrate myself, that they also may be sanctified in truth.
>
> **JOHN 17:14-19**

What stands out to you about Jesus' prayer for the disciples?

Jesus gave a very simple equation in verse 17: God's Word = truth. Is this a difficult concept for you to accept? How do you think most people in the culture you live in would define *truth*?

Twice Jesus asked God to sanctify the disciples in the truth. In both cases the disciples were the passive recipients of that sanctification. God is the One who sanctifies believers by His truth.

God gave us His Word in the first place, and He's the One who sanctifies us through it. What's our role in the process of sanctification through God's Word? What's our contribution?

Jesus' prayer for us to be sanctified in the truth is for us to be transformed in every sense of the word. It's possible that the Lord was praying specifically for the disciples who would launch the global church, but it's likely that this prayer covers all disciples of all time. It would be answered in the lives of disciples for millennia, so we're now the recipients of this powerful prayer. Jesus prayed that our lives would be saturated with the truth. Because this is the will of God, we can dive into the Word of God with gospel confidence that the Spirit is working the Word into our hearts and minds for God's desired ends.

I've received iTunes gift cards on several occasions. While the card enables me to access an amazing array of resources, I don't have access to what I want until I log in. I can't download any music, movies, or television shows unless I log in and gain access. Faith is the login for our access to the Word of God through the gospel. Reading, meditating, memorizing, preaching, hearing, attending Bible studies—we must pursue all these outlets to gain access to God's Word.

To what extent have you logged in and started downloading what God has to say in His Word? If the scale below were a progress bar on your computer showing how much of the Bible you've downloaded (read), how far along would you be? Shade in your progress.

0%   100%

In what ways do you expose yourself to God's Word? List them here.

What are some new ways you might be able to incorporate the Bible into your life?

Jesus' assertion that God's Word is the truth wasn't a new idea. If the disciples listening to Jesus knew their Old Testaments well, they would have also known what the psalmist wrote in Psalm 119:

[159]Consider how I love your precepts!
  Give me life according to your steadfast love.
[160]The sum of your word is truth,
  and every one of your righteous rules endures forever.
PSALM 119:159-160

What stands out to you about these verses?

**To what extent would you say that you love God's precepts (His Word)?
What can you do to increase your love for the Bible?**

**What's the significance of verse 160? How does this verse affect your motivation
to read the Bible regularly?**

Finish this section of study by praying this prayer:

Heavenly Father, I thank You that You've revealed Yourself to me through Your Word. I thank You that You didn't remain a mystery to me. You allowed Your vision for my life to come to me in written form so that I'd know who You are and how to live a life that honors You. Help me have the perspective that all of Your Word is useful for my life. Show me that the Bible plays a holy, indescribably important role in my sanctification. Help me never to lose that perspective. Cultivate in me the attitude that Your Word is a light shining into my life and into the world. Show me what it looks like to digest and apply more of Your Word in my life. I love You, Lord, and I thank You for Your holy Word. Amen.

*Unlike human beings, who can utter
thousands on thousands of words to no
effect, when God speaks, things happen.*
#UNLEASHED

DIGGING DEEPER

Criminals are dangerous because they disregard the law. Laws (for the most part) are put in place to establish order in society. Without laws, the result is anarchy, violence, and suffering. Law exists in the natural sphere because sin exists, and sin foments disorder. The presence of law assumes the sinfulness of man. If man were governed by God's character, there would be no need for law.

Just as human laws point out the sinfulness of man, so does divine law. We can't understand the Word of God without understanding the role of the law established in the Old Testament and Jesus' fulfillment of the law in the New Testament. The law exposes sin, which stunts our spiritual growth. We can't grow in sanctification if we're lawless people. Paul wrote:

> What then shall we say? That the law is sin? By no means!
> Yet if it had not been for the law, I would not have known sin.
> **ROMANS 7:7**

While showing man to be sinful, the law reveals the holiness of the living God. Are we under the law? No, but it's still profitable for doctrine (see 2 Tim. 3:16). We can't appreciate Jesus Christ if we don't appreciate the law He came to fulfill. So to appreciate the law is to revere Jesus. The law makes us see our need for mercy and transformation through the gospel. As we see our need for mercy, we're driven to the gospel. That's why Paul said:

> We know that the law is good, if one uses it lawfully, understanding
> this, that the law is not laid down for the just but for the lawless and
> disobedient, for the ungodly and sinners, for the unholy and profane, for
> those who strike their fathers and mothers, for murderers, the sexually
> immoral, men who practice homosexuality, enslavers, liars, perjurers,
> and whatever else is contrary to sound doctrine, in accordance with the
> gospel of the glory of the blessed God with which I have been entrusted.
> **1 TIMOTHY 1:8-11**

In other words, the law helps us all see our sin. We can't confess our sin unless we clearly see our sin. So we can't be sanctified according to God's plan unless we understand sin according to the law in the Word of God.

What has your view of the law been up until this point in your faith journey?

Why do you think it's important for Christ followers to understand the Old Testament law?

Jesus said He didn't come to abolish the law but to fulfill it (see Matt. 5:17-18). What do you think He meant?

All people think, act, form values, and have affections that are all shaped by the way we filter everything we experience. Some call this filter a worldview. I define *worldview* as *a grid through which followers of Jesus Christ view; interact with; and understand God, people, and the world.* It's important to understand that mind renewal doesn't happen by osmosis but by intentional interaction with the Word of God. The Holy Spirit applies God's Word to us, but we have to do the hard work of being in places where the Word is dispensed. To be doers of the Word, we must be hearers of the Word (see Jas. 1:22).

Romans 12 calls us to renew our minds:

> I appeal to you therefore, brothers, by the mercies of God, to present
> your bodies as a living sacrifice, holy and acceptable to God, which
> is your spiritual worship. Do not be conformed to this world, but be
> transformed by the renewal of your mind, that by testing you may discern
> what is the will of God, what is good and acceptable and perfect.
> **ROMANS 12:1-2**

Mind renewal is at the core of sanctification. If change happens in our minds, it will happen in every other part of the body. Mind and heart, in terms of biblical sanctification, are the same thing. Both point to the core of who we are. In our hearts and minds lie our hopes, dreams, and beliefs. If we aren't changed on that level, our lives remain captive to our natural way of thinking and are deeply vulnerable to the Devil. God's truth sets us free (see John 8:32).

List three things you can remove from your life that might be impeding the renewal of your mind (for example, TV shows, social media, certain friends, etc.).

What are three things you could add to your life that would help in the process of renewing your mind?

Why do you think renewing your mind based on God's Word will help you discern the will of God?

How is renewing your mind according to God's standards an act of "spiritual worship" (see Rom. 12:1)?

Consider the first words in the Book of Psalms. They highlight the need to delight in God's Word and allow it to change us:

> Blessed is the man
> who walks not in the counsel of the wicked,
> nor stands in the way of sinners,
> nor sits in the seat of scoffers;
> but his delight is in the law of the LORD,
> and on his law he meditates day and night.
> He is like a tree
> planted by streams of water
> that yields its fruit in its season,
> and its leaf does not wither.
> In all that he does, he prospers.
> The wicked are not so,
> but are like chaff that the wind drives away.
> Therefore the wicked will not stand in the judgment,
> nor sinners in the congregation of the righteous;
> for the LORD knows the way of the righteous,
> but the way of the wicked will perish.
> **PSALM 1**

This psalm talks about a blessed person. Go back and circle the things this blessed person does. Then underline the benefits of those actions.

Now strike through the things the blessed person is supposed to avoid. Note the consequences if he or she doesn't avoid these things.

Review the marks you made and think about this passage in terms of your own sanctification. What are your observations?

The psalmist stated that people who experience the greatest amount of sustainable joy and happiness are those who find intense pleasure and satisfaction in the Word of God. In other words, when we delight in God's Word, the blessedness of verse 1 enters every area of our experience.

Let's look at another psalm that reflects on God's Word and its importance for our lives and our sanctification:

> [89]Forever, O LORD, your word
>   is firmly fixed in the heavens.
> [90]Your faithfulness endures to all generations;
>   you have established the earth, and it stands fast.
> [91]By your appointment they stand this day,
>   for all things are your servants.
> [92]If your law had not been my delight,
>   I would have perished in my affliction.
> [93]I will never forget your precepts,
>   for by them you have given me life.
> [94]I am yours; save me,
>   for I have sought your precepts.
> [95]The wicked lie in wait to destroy me,
>   but I consider your testimonies.
> [96]I have seen a limit to all perfection,
>   but your commandment is exceedingly broad.
> [97]Oh how I love your law!
>   It is my meditation all the day.
> [98]Your commandment makes me wiser than my enemies,
>   for it is ever with me.
> [99]I have more understanding than all my teachers,
>   for your testimonies are my meditation.

¹⁰⁰I understand more than the aged,
    for I keep your precepts.
¹⁰¹I hold back my feet from every evil way,
    in order to keep your word.
¹⁰²I do not turn aside from your rules,
    for you have taught me.
¹⁰³How sweet are your words to my taste,
    sweeter than honey to my mouth!
¹⁰⁴Through your precepts I get understanding;
    therefore I hate every false way.
¹⁰⁵Your word is a lamp to my feet
    and a light to my path.

PSALM 119:89-105

Circle every word in this passage that refers to God's Word.

List the benefits of knowing God's Word, according to this passage.

What stands out to you in this passage? Which descriptions do you wish were true of your life, and how can you work on these?

Do you consider God's Word to be "sweet," as the psalmist described in verse 103? Would you be able to say the words "I love your law!" (v. 97)? What stands in your way of being able to view God's Word that way?

What words would you choose to describe your view of God's Word?

In the final Scripture passage we'll hear from the prophet Isaiah on the power of God's Word. Isaiah casts a vision for why we should seek God's Word:

As the rain and the snow come down from heaven
    and do not return there but water the earth,
making it bring forth and sprout,   giving seed
to the sower and bread to the eater,
so shall my word be that goes out from my mouth;
    it shall not return to me empty,
but it shall accomplish that which I purpose,
    and shall succeed in the thing for which I sent it.
ISAIAH 55:10-11

What stands out to you in this text?

What does this passage add to your view of God's Word?

God's Word is powerful. It doesn't return void but accomplishes what God wants it to accomplish. That being the case, we must seek to know as much of His Word as possible and seek to hear His voice through our personal relationship with Christ. In doing so, we'll experience growth in Christlikeness.

Finish this section of study by praying this prayer:

Dear Lord, I want to have a genuine love for Your Word. I want to delight in it. Sometimes I don't feel that way, and often Your Word is relegated to the back burner of my busy life. I'm sorry for that, Lord, and I need Your help to change it. I want to be like the blessed person of Psalm 1, yielding fruit like a tree planted near streams of water. I want to be that tree, Lord, continually nourished and fed by Your Word so that I can bear the fruit You want me to bear and grow to be more and more like your Son, Jesus. Amen.

Mind renewal doesn't happen by osmosis but by intentional interaction with the Word of God.
#UNLEASHED

GOSPEL APPLICATION

In our study this week we've seen that God's Word is critical to our spiritual growth and an inseparable part of our lives as Christ followers. We must regularly engage with God's Word in order to grow closer to God and become more like Jesus. In this final lesson we'll look at four ways we can allow God's Word to change our hearts and minds: hearing the Word, receiving the Word, studying the Word, and meditating on the Word.

HEARING THE WORD

Hearing God's Word requires that we put ourselves in the path of those who are speaking the Word. It means we don't forsake gathering together for the preaching of the Word. It means we load up our iPhones with sermons that expose the Word. It means we stand shoulder to shoulder with the people at the mission who sit under the preaching of a gospel evangelist. It means we discipline ourselves to make sure our path intersects with the Word wherever it's being preached.

Consider what the author of Hebrews had to say about hearing God's Word:

> Let us hold fast the confession of our hope without wavering,
> for he who promised is faithful. And let us consider how to
> stir up one another to love and good works, not neglecting to
> meet together, as is the habit of some, but encouraging one
> another, and all the more as you see the Day drawing near.
> **HEBREWS 10:23-25**

How does hearing God's Word help us "hold fast the confession of our hope without wavering" (v. 23)?

The writer of Hebrews warned his readers not to neglect meeting together (for the purpose of hearing the Word), and then he mentioned that some people make a habit of missing the gatherings of the body of Christ.

Why do you think many Christians struggle with consistently gathering with others at church? Have you struggled with this? Why or why not?

In His famous parable of the sower (see Mark 4:3-9), Jesus described four ways to hear and respond to God's Word. After telling the parable, Jesus said to His listeners, "He who has ears to hear, let him hear" (v. 9). His disciples wanted to make sure they'd truly heard Jesus, so they asked him to explain the parable to them. Jesus explained it this way:

> The sower sows the word. And these are the ones along the path, where the word is sown: when they hear, Satan immediately comes and takes away the word that is sown in them. And these are the ones sown on rocky ground: the ones who, when they hear the word, immediately receive it with joy. And they have no root in themselves, but endure for a while; then, when tribulation or persecution arises on account of the word, immediately they fall away. And others are the ones sown among thorns. They are those who hear the word, but the cares of the world and the deceitfulness of riches and the desires for other things enter in and choke the word, and it proves unfruitful. But those that were sown on the good soil are the ones who hear the word and accept it and bear fruit, thirtyfold and sixtyfold and a hundredfold.
>
> **MARK 4:14-20**

List the four types of soil Jesus described in this parable.

Record times in your life when you've been each type of soil through your action or attitude.

During times when you've been good soil, what habits allowed you to hear the Word, accept it, and bear fruit? How can you replicate those behaviors in your life now?

Merely hearing the Word isn't the end goal. Hearing the Word is always for the purpose of doing the will of God, as we'll see. Truly hearing the Word is one of the main entryways to be sanctified by the Word of God. Because our hearts are changed by the gospel, believers in Jesus are good soil.

RECEIVING THE WORD

If the purpose of hearing the Word is to expose us to the Word, the purpose of receiving the Word is to internalize what we hear. It's one thing to hear God's Word, but it's another thing to receive by faith what it says. James placed hearing and receiving in the same context to make this idea clear to us:

Be doers of the word, and not hearers only, deceiving yourselves. For if anyone is a hearer of the word and not a doer, he is like a man who looks intently at his natural face in a mirror. For he looks at himself and goes away and at once forgets what he was like. But the one who looks into the perfect law, the law of liberty, and perseveres, being no hearer who forgets but a doer who acts, he will be blessed in his doing.

JAMES 1:22-25

Which is more challenging to you—consistently hearing the Word or following through and acting on it?

In what ways have you forgotten what you look like? That is, you've acted in a way you know is counter to your Christian faith?

Why do you think James emphasized the importance of doing the Word? What's the risk of only hearing the Word and not acting on it?

It's possible to be a hearer without being a receiver, but we can't be a receiver and not a hearer. Yet more broadly, true hearing is receiving, which leads to doing. This is how we participate in God's plan to grow us in Christlikeness. We not only hear the Word but also receive the Word by putting it into practice.

STUDYING THE WORD

As a pastor, I'm sensitive to the pressing, practical needs in a congregation. Sermons and every area of pastoral ministry ought to be aimed at meeting those needs. In my sermon preparation I'm always pondering my responsibility, by the power of the Spirit, to connect the Scriptures to real life. However, I find that the average Christian is bored and closed to learning what's necessary for a walk of faith. Many of us are more concerned about God's meeting our needs than about knowing and loving Him. So we shirk the responsibility to study God's Word. But God's Word is living and active. It speaks to us like no other book, blog, or tweet, and we need to read it in a consistent, focused way to grow closer to God:

The word of God is living and active, sharper than any two-edged sword, piercing to the division of soul and of spirit, of joints and of marrow, and discerning the thoughts and intentions of the heart.

HEBREWS 4:12

This verse describes God's Word as sharp and piercing, able to discern the inner thoughts and intentions of the heart. How in your own study of God's Word have you seen the work of this deeply penetrating source of truth?

As important as devotional insights are, we need to have the rich nutrients of the Word implanted deep within us in order to grow. That gospel growth is the means God uses to answer our prayers, meet our needs, and fix our problems. Believers need to study the Word and grow in the knowledge of the heart and mind of Christ.

Read 2 Timothy 2:15. What importance does the last part of the verse have for the first part?

The point of this verse is the presentation of oneself to God, which is the only way to communicate God's Word with accuracy. With this imperative in mind, all believers should make it a priority to be built up with an accurate understanding of God's Word that comes from careful study.

God's Word needs to be the object of our consistent attention. We need not only to hear and think about it but also to be active in studying it and discovering its full significance. There's simply no other book like it.

MEDITATING ON THE WORD

As many Christian teachers have said on this subject, the church has let Eastern religions hijack one of the most powerful means of grace for spiritual growth. In contrast with the Eastern practice, however, Christian meditation isn't clearing or emptying our minds but filling our minds with God's Word. Meditation develops our ability to absorb God's Word.

The Book of Psalms talks a lot about delighting in God's Word. The word *delight* in the psalms characterizes meditation that flows from memorization. If we delight in something, we store the knowledge of it within us. To delight in the Word, we must have a continual relationship with it; we must store knowledge of the Word in our hearts. Reflecting on David's words in the psalms, Spurgeon wrote:

> "The law of the Lord" is the daily bread of the true believer. And yet, in David's day, how small was the volume of inspiration, for they had scarcely anything save the first five books of Moses! How much more, then, should we prize the whole written Word which it is our privilege to have in all our houses![1]

What do you think about Spurgeon's words? What stands out to you?

Do you feel that God's Word is your daily bread—that you'll go spiritually hungry if you don't partake of the Bible each day?

In Acts 17 Paul and his coworkers in ministry were traveling through Greece, bringing the gospel to that part of the world for the first time. Forcefully driven out of Thessalonica, a city in northern Greece, Paul and Silas next went to the town of Berea. Here's what Luke wrote about the Paul's interaction with the Bereans:

> The brothers immediately sent Paul and Silas away by night to Berea, and when they arrived they went into the Jewish synagogue. Now these Jews were more noble than those in Thessalonica; they received the word with all eagerness, examining the Scriptures daily to see if these things were so. Many of them therefore believed, with not a few Greek women of high standing as well as men.
> ACTS 17:10-12

According to Luke, what made the Bereans more noble than the Thessalonians?

What can we learn from the Bereans' example?

What habits can you adopt to cultivate the instincts the Bereans had?

The Bereans were earnestly seeking the truth, and they searched the Scriptures to find it. Our spiritual lives should be filled with moments of red-hot pursuit of the Lord, times when we diligently search God's Word for the truth that will enable us to grow closer to God. A continual engagement with God's Word should be a hallmark of our lives, something others notice about us. Paul said it this way:

Let the word of Christ dwell in you richly, teaching and admonishing
one another in all wisdom, singing psalms and hymns and
spiritual songs, with thankfulness in your hearts to God.

COLOSSIANS 3:16

Letting the Word richly dwell in us is done through meditation. Our meditation doesn't make improvements on the Word, but it increases the intensity of our absorption of the Word. As our minds are plunged into the Word through constant, repetitive meditation, we find ourselves saturated. As we muse on, consider, think on, ponder, and give serious consideration to information or a situation in the Bible, we take the Word very seriously. To let the Word dwell richly within us is to realize the depth of the Word.

A CALL TO ACTION

To unleash the power of the Spirit of God that conforms us to the image of Christ, we have to unleash the Word of God in our lives. We must hear the Word, receive the Word, study and know the Word, and meditate on the Word.

A popular quotation attributed to Spurgeon says:

> The Word of God is like a lion. You don't have to defend a lion. All you have to do is let the lion loose, and the lion will defend itself.[2]

Finish this lesson by composing a prayer to God. Ask Him to open your mind and heart to His Word. Tell Him your intentions for hearing, receiving, studying, and meditating on His Word more consistently. Finally, praise God for giving you access to the truth of Scripture, God's revelation of Himself.

1. Charles Spurgeon, "The Treasury of David," *The Spurgeon Archive* [online, cited 4 December 2015]. Available from the Internet: *www.spurgeon.org.*
2. Charles Spurgeon, *All About God* [online], 15 September 2009 [cited 4 December 2015]. Available from the Internet: *www.allaboutgod.net.*

*A continual engagement with God's
Word should be a hallmark of our lives,
something others notice about us.*

#UNLEASHED

GROWN THROUGH PRAYER

START

Welcome to session 5 of *Unleashed*. Open the group session by asking participants to discuss the following questions.

> As you completed this week's personal study, what did the Lord show you? How did He speak to you?

> What role do you believe prayer plays in your spiritual growth? How have you experienced closeness to God through prayer?

> Why do you think establishing or maintaining a regular routine of prayer is challenging for most of us?

Prayer is one of those disciplines we all struggle with. Every Christian agrees we should pray. Most Christians want to have a vibrant prayer life, even if they struggle to develop one. But most of us have difficulty prioritizing prayer in our lives and establishing a workable, meaningful habit of prayer. Our general lack of consistency in our prayer lives reveals that many of us don't understand the function of prayer and the ways God uses prayer to grow us in intimacy with Him and in ever-increasing likeness to Jesus.

Today we'll hear Pastor Mason discuss the important subject of prayer and the way God uses our prayer lives to sanctify us. He will bring clarity to God's desires for our prayer lives and will help us calibrate our view of prayer to the biblical ideal.

Watch video session 5, in which Pastor Mason helps us understand the vital role of prayer in our sanctification.

WATCH

> In the days of his flesh, Jesus offered up prayers and supplications, with loud cries and tears, to him who was able to save him from death, and he was heard because of his reverence. Although he was a son, he learned obedience through what he suffered. And being made perfect, he became the source of eternal salvation to all who obey him, being designated by God a high priest after the order of Melchizedek.
>
> **HEBREWS 5:7-10**

> Draw near to God, and he will draw near to you.
>
> **JAMES 4:8**

> Since then we have a great high priest who has passed through the heavens, Jesus, the Son of God, let us hold fast our confession. For we do not have a high priest who is unable to sympathize with our weaknesses, but one who in every respect has been tempted as we are, yet without sin. Let us then with confidence draw near to the throne of grace, that we may receive mercy and find grace to help in time of need.
>
> **HEBREWS 4:14-16**

> Since, therefore, we have now been justified by his blood, much more shall we be saved by him from the wrath of God.
>
> **ROMANS 5:9**

RESPOND

In this session Pastor Mason helped us understand the vital role of prayer in our relationship with God and in our sanctification.

What stood out to you in this session?

What struggles have you faced as you've tried to establish a consistent, meaningful prayer life?

What does it mean to you to know that Jesus Himself had an active prayer life?

As the writer of Hebrews stated, we can approach God in prayer with confidence.

Have you ever thought about the fact that God has invited you into His throne room through prayer? How does this reality affect your view of God?

Pastor Mason said prayer is a process of aligning our lives with God's will, not dictating to Him what we want Him to do for us.

How does this understanding change your view of prayer?

What did you find most inspiring in this video session? What step will you take to strengthen your prayer life?

In closing, pray and thank God for inviting us to have an intimate relationship with Him through prayer and for making the throne of grace available to us through Jesus. Also ask Him to cultivate in you a desire for prayer and the self-discipline necessary to consistently pray. Ask Him to use your prayer life to grow you in conformity to His Son.

Complete the following three personal-study sections before the next group session. One section will focus on this week's big idea, the next section will dig deeper into Scripture, and the final section will focus on application.

THE BIG IDEA

As easy as prayer may seem, it can be the most difficult spiritual discipline in our lives. We see celebrities pray at award shows, athletes pray when they achieve their goals, and fictional characters pray in movies when their situation seems beyond their own power. And prayer is often the first step of faith for a new believer—the first thing we do when we believe and are transformed by the gospel.

Prayer seems easy because it is. But to have the sort of prayer life that unleashes the sanctifying power of the Spirit in our lives requires more than pointing up to heaven in the end zone after a touchdown. Like every other aspect of sanctification, it requires God's help. We can't grow spiritually through prayer without God's speaking to us and showing us more of Himself through it.

Simply put, prayer is having a conversation with God—speaking to him about our lives and intently listening for His voice. We all have access to the living God through Jesus Christ in prayer, and it's critical that we have a vibrant, consistent prayer life in order to be conformed more and more to the image of Christ.

Imagine you're reviewing your prayer life on Yelp or Amazon. How many stars would you give it, and what would your review say? Color in the number of stars for your review.

Write your review here. My prayer life is:

In what ways do you wish your prayer life would change?

How do you think a vibrant prayer life would help you draw closer to God?

Prayer is everywhere in the New Testament. Almost every book of the New Testament contains prayer or at least a reference to it. From the larger books like Romans and Luke to the smaller ones like Philemon and Jude, prayer is present. God made sure His revelation to humanity included instruction on how to pray.

As you read prayers in the Bible, you begin to see that many of them pertain to spiritual growth. It's clear that prayer is a core component of our growth that the Spirit uses to transform us into the likeness of our Lord Jesus.

So what exactly happens when we pray? What's prayer supposed to achieve, and how should we view it? There are three key purposes for prayer: deeper fellowship with God, alignment with God's will, and intercession on behalf of others.

DEEPER FELLOWSHIP WITH GOD

Prayer is the chamber in which a sinner-turned-saint builds deeper fellowship with God. There's no better example of this pursuit than the Lord's Prayer, in which Jesus taught His followers how God wants them to pray. Jesus said:

> Pray then like this:
> Our Father in heaven,
> hallowed be your name.
> Your kingdom come,
> your will be done,
>   on earth as it is in heaven.
> Give us this day our daily bread,
> and forgive us our debts,
>   as we also have forgiven our debtors.
> And lead us not into temptation,
>   but deliver us from evil.
> **MATTHEW 6:9-13**

What do you notice about this prayer?

What surprises you about the way Jesus said to pray?

How does this prayer resemble your prayers, and how is it different?

Jesus said to "pray then like this" (v. 9), meaning we aren't supposed to simply recite this prayer verbatim but to use it as a pattern. What principles or themes do you observe in this prayer that you could incorporate into your prayer life?

How do you think praying like this would increase your fellowship with God?

When we survey all of Scripture, we see that prayer takes many forms, including the elements we just saw in the Lord's Prayer. Prayer include confessing, repenting, extolling God's majesty, venting, and just enjoying God's presence.

Our prayer lives must be driven by these elements as we engage with God in prayer. Most of our prayers have as their goal growing deeper in our relationship with God. No matter how short or long our prayers are, we must make them part of our daily regimen so that we can continually grow closer to God by talking and listening to Him.

ALIGNMENT WITH GOD'S WILL

When we pray often enough not only to speak to God but also to listen to Him, we realize that our will and God's will often come into conflict with each other. We detect a difference between what we want and what God wants for our lives. I'll let you speculate about who's going to win that wrestling match.

Many of us don't pray enough to wrestle with our King. If we're going to be sanctified by God, if we're going to grow more and more into the image of Christ, we mustn't be strangers to heaven's throne of grace. A life marked by disciplined prayer conforms our will to the will of God, and we become people who are always ready to say, "Not my will, but yours, be done" (Luke 22:42).

Do you remember the context of that quotation? Jesus was praying in the garden of Gethsemane on the eve of His arrest, trial, and crucifixion. Agonizing over the suffering He'd endure and the separation from God He'd experience, He prayed to align His heart with God's will. Luke described the dramatic scene:

> [Jesus] withdrew from them about a stone's throw, and knelt
> down and prayed, saying, "Father, if you are willing, remove this
> cup from me. Nevertheless, not my will, but yours, be done." And
> there appeared to him an angel from heaven, strengthening him.
> And being in an agony he prayed more earnestly; and his sweat
> became like great drops of blood falling down to the ground.
> **LUKE 22:41-44**

What stands out to you about this passage?

What does it mean to you to know that Jesus Himself prayed for God's will to come to pass, in spite of His own feelings of dread?

Identify a situation in your life that was so difficult or painful that it was hard to pray for God's will to be done.

When we truly listen to God in prayer and respond in obedience to His revelation to us, our hearts and lives begin to come into alignment with His will.

INTERCESSION ON BEHALF OF OTHERS

Finally, we pray to benefit others. We lift up others in prayer when they're going through difficulty or need God's guidance in a special way. Intercession is the most sacrificial type of prayer because it involves growing in Christlike empathy for the needs of others.

Jesus stated several times that He was praying for the growth of His disciples (see Luke 22:32; John 17). As a matter of fact, His major ministry on our behalf at the right hand of God is to intercede for us (see Rom. 8:34). Part of being conformed to the image of Christ means praying the way He prayed through the ministry of intercession. Paul described this incredible reality in one of the most magnificent passages in all of his writings:

> Who shall bring any charge against God's elect? It is God who justifies. Who is to condemn? Christ Jesus is the one who died—more than that, who was raised—who is at the right hand of God, who indeed is interceding for us. Who shall separate us from the love of Christ? Shall tribulation, or distress, or persecution, or famine, or nakedness, or danger, or sword? As it is written,
> "For your sake we are being killed all the day long;
> we are regarded as sheep to be slaughtered."
> No, in all these things we are more than conquerors through him who loved us. For I am sure that neither death nor life, nor angels nor rulers, nor things present nor things to come, nor powers, nor height nor depth, nor anything else in all creation, will be able to separate us from the love of God in Christ Jesus our Lord.
> **ROMANS 8:33-39**

The risen Christ, seated at the right hand God, intercedes for you. How does this truth affect your faith?

Why do you think Paul went on to state that we can never be separated from Christ? What's the relationship between Christ's intercession and our sanctification?

How does this passage inspire you to intercede for other people in prayer?

Intercession for others can be applied not only individually but also corporately. One of the first things the disciples did after receiving the Holy Spirit in Acts 2 was to pray together (see v. 42). The Spirit desires to conform the entire body of Christ to His image as we pray together.

Finish this section of study by praying this prayer:

Lord, I thank You that You allow me to grow in my relationship with You through prayer. I ask that You'll use my times of prayer to grow closer to You and to become more and more like Your Son. Help me listen as much as I speak, and help me pray for others as much as I pray for myself. I pray, Father, that You'll lead me to seek Your will and not my own. Help me establish habits and routines in my life that yield a consistent, vibrant prayer life. I pray that You'll sanctify me through that process. Continually remind that You, Jesus, are interceding for me at the right hand of God. Strengthen and encourage me by that knowledge and give me security in realizing that I can never be separated from You. I also ask, Lord, that Your intercession for me will inspire me to be an intercessor for others. Sanctify me, Lord, through my prayer life. Lead me into refreshing times of fellowship with You and grow me through them. Amen.

Prayer is the chamber in which a sinner-turned-saint builds deeper fellowship with God.
#UNLEASHED

DIGGING DEEPER

When I received discipline from my parents, it was extremely difficult, to say the very least. My parents were hard-core disciplinarians. But in many ways these experiences were helpful for me. By being consistently disciplined, I never wondered where the boundaries were. Though I continued to behave in ways that warranted strong discipline, I always knew what was acceptable and what wasn't.

On the other hand, I often didn't know when I was restored to fellowship with my parents. My punishments didn't have time limits, so I didn't know when I'd regain the privileges I'd lost through discipline. Though the boundaries of transgression were clear, the conditions of restoration were unclear. It was difficult to know when I could once again draw near to them.

One major point the Bible drives home is the fact that we always have access to God through the Lord Jesus Christ, and one of the major access points in that relationship is our prayer life. For instance, the Book of Hebrews was written to show that our access to Christ is far superior to prior means of access to God. The theme of drawing near to God is a constant refrain in the book, with the term "Draw near" occurring 19 times. The way we draw near to God is most often understood as coming to Him in prayer.

One of the most memorable verses expressing that theme is:

Let us then with confidence draw near to the throne of grace,
that we may receive mercy and find grace to help in time of need.
HEBREWS 4:16

Why do you think the author of Hebrews emphasized confidence in this verse?

Think about the phrase "throne of grace." How can that phrase be considered a radical concept?

That verse is pretty incredible on its own, but to interpret Scripture accurately, we need to consider the context. Let's back up a few verses:

> [14]Since then we have a great high priest who has passed through the heavens, Jesus, the Son of God, let us hold fast our confession. [15]For we do not have a high priest who is unable to sympathize with our weaknesses, but one who in every respect has been tempted as we are, yet without sin. [16]Let us then with confidence draw near to the throne of grace, that we may receive mercy and find grace to help in time of need.
>
> **HEBREWS 4:14-16**

According to the writer of Hebrews, Jesus is our Great High Priest, who is far superior to any human high priest. Having experienced life as a human, He understands what we go through. He intercedes for us with that human understanding and with divine power as the Son of God.

What do verses 14-15 add to your understanding of verse 16? How do they or should they affect your prayer life?

Later in Hebrews the writer expanded on this concept of Jesus as our High Priest:

> The former priests were many in number, because they were prevented by death from continuing in office, but [Jesus] holds his priesthood permanently, because he continues forever. Consequently, he is able to save to the uttermost those who draw near to God through him, since he always lives to make intercession for them. For it was indeed fitting that we should have such a high priest, holy, innocent, unstained, separated from sinners, and exalted above the heavens. He has no need, like those high priests, to offer sacrifices daily, first for his own sins and then for those of the people, since he did this once for all when he offered up himself.
>
> **HEBREWS 7:23-27**

According to this text, why is Jesus a superior High Priest to the earthly priests of Israel?

How does this passage change your view of who Christ is? How does it affect your prayer life?

Our ability to approach God's throne is a mind-blowing reality. It's hard for us today to comprehend the depth of this imagery because we don't live under the rule of a monarch. We have to understand the Kingdom imagery of the Bible to grasp what the writer of Hebrews meant. These words from C. E. Arnold can help us gain some perspective on the monumental blessing of being able to draw near to the throne of God:

> Monarchs of the ancient world sat on thrones as symbols of their power and authority. Consequently, to approach a monarch's throne could be a fearsome act, for one was at the mercy of the ruler, who had the power of life and death in hand. The throne imagery also carried over into religious beliefs. ... When used with reference to the gods, a throne also was a symbol of power and authority. In Christian belief God's throne is a seat of authority and power, but, as Hebrews points out, it too is a seat of grace. Thus, the believer who has Christ as his high priest can approach the throne with "confidence" or boldness. In Hellenistic Judaism and early Christianity the concept of drawing near to God with confidence refers especially to approaching God in prayer.[1]

How does Arnold's description illuminate the previous Hebrews text?

What words would you use to describe monarchs? How do those words contrast with the throne of Christ?

How would you explain the lordship of Christ to someone who's new to the faith or someone who's exploring Christianity? How could you use this throne imagery to help them understand who Jesus is?

Coming to the throne of an earthly ruler might not naturally inspire confidence. It might be dangerous to approach the throne. The king might not be willing to grant the requests of his subjects. Maybe the king has a habit of humiliating people who approach with requests. But the Lord Jesus communicates in Hebrews 4:16 that we should approach the King of all creation with confidence.

This invitation is all the more remarkable considering the fact that God, in His infinite power, is worthy of our fear—deep respect for His divine authority. In fact, many Old Testament writings say the fear of the Lord is a prerequisite for spiritual growth. For example, Moses said this when the Israelites were about to enter the promised land:

> This is the commandment—the statutes and the rules—that the
> LORD your God commanded me to teach you, that you may do them
> in the land to which you are going over, to possess it, that you may
> fear the LORD your God, you and your son and your son's son, by
> keeping all his statutes and his commandments, which I command
> you, all the days of your life, and that your days may be long.
>
> **DEUTERONOMY 6:1-2**

Similarly, Moses' protégé and successor, Joshua, said this after leading the Israelites into the promised land:

> Fear the LORD and serve him in sincerity and in faithfulness. Put away
> the gods that your fathers served beyond the River and in Egypt, and
> serve the LORD. And if it is evil in your eyes to serve the LORD, choose
> this day whom you will serve, whether the gods your fathers served
> in the region beyond the River, or the gods of the Amorites in whose
> land you dwell. But as for me and my house, we will serve the LORD.
>
> **JOSHUA 24:14-15**

Why do you think it was important for the people of Israel to live in fear of the Lord—to have a deep sense of His power and majesty?

Why is it important for us to have a healthy fear of the Lord?

The Books of Psalms and Proverbs consistently mention the fear of the Lord as an integral part of our sanctification. Take some time to reflect on these examples and jot down any lessons they hold for your spiritual growth.

Let all the earth fear the LORD;
let all the inhabitants of the world stand in awe of him!
PSALM 33:8

The fear of the LORD is the beginning of knowledge;
fools despise wisdom and instruction.
PROVERBS 1:7

My son, if you receive my words
and treasure up my commandments with you,
making your ear attentive to wisdom
and inclining your heart to understanding;
yes, if you call out for insight
and raise your voice for understanding,
if you seek it like silver
and search for it as for hidden treasures,
then you will understand the fear of the LORD
and find the knowledge of God.
For the LORD gives wisdom;
from his mouth come knowledge and understanding.
PROVERBS 2:1-6

Everyone who is arrogant in heart is an abomination to the LORD;
be assured, he will not go unpunished.
By steadfast love and faithfulness iniquity is atoned for,
and by the fear of the LORD one turns away from evil.
PROVERBS 16:5-6

The fear of the LORD leads to life,
and whoever has it rests satisfied;
he will not be visited by harm.
PROVERBS 19:23

Because Jesus has given His life for our sin and has become our Great High Priest in heaven, we have access to the presence of the King before whom we'd otherwise be unable to stand. We can have an appropriate fear of God while simultaneously having confidence in our ability to draw near to Him. God's wrath, which ought to be exercised on every subject in the Kingdom who sought to subvert His rule, has been satisfied by the death of Christ. Since God's wrath has been extinguished, we don't approach God's throne as people who are worthy of wrath but as recipients of grace. Christ stood before the throne on our behalf, absorbed God's wrath, and took all the punishment for our sin so that we can draw near to God in confidence that He accepts us as holy and righteous.

We now come as court officials, princes, brothers of the King, and inheritors of the Kingdom when we make our requests in prayer. We approach with confidence because there's no longer anything to be afraid of. The King invites us to approach the throne, sinful though we are, and talk to Him.

It seems to be a contradiction to say we can approach God with both confidence and fear. Relying on the ideas you've learned in this section of study, explain how believers are able to approach the throne of grace with both.

Finish this section of study by praying this prayer:

Lord, I pray that You'll sanctify my mind to think rightly about You, teaching me to have appropriate fear of and reverence for You. Through my standing in the righteousness of Jesus, give me confidence to approach your throne of grace through prayer. Help me always be awed by the magnitude of my ability to approach You directly through the work of Your Son. Help me always recognize prayer as the indescribable blessing it is. Amen.

1. Clinton E. Arnold, gen. ed., *Zondervan Illustrated Bible Backgrounds Commentary*, vol. 4, *Hebrews to Revelation* (Grand Rapids, MI: Zondervan, 2002), 31.

> *Since God's wrath has been extinguished, we don't approach God's throne as people who are worthy of wrath but as recipients of grace.*
> #UNLEASHED

GOSPEL APPLICATION

This week we've been studying prayer and its role in our sanctification. Prayer is one of the most vital tools for our growth in Christlikeness. God uses it in a powerful way to draw us closer to Him.

It may surprise you to know that God used prayer in the life of His Son, Jesus, while He was on earth. For example, Hebrews 5:7-9 says:

> In the days of his flesh, Jesus offered up prayers and supplications, with loud cries and tears, to him who was able to save him from death, and he was heard because of his reverence. Although he was a son, he learned obedience through what he suffered. And being made perfect, he became the source of eternal salvation to all who obey him.
>
> **HEBREWS 5:7-9**

These verses make clear that prayer was a huge part of Jesus' learning process. Even though Jesus was born perfect in both His humanity and His divine nature, He learned in His humanity. The words "learned obedience" (v. 8) mean that in His humanity Jesus submitted to growth. I won't begin to try to explain this mystery, but Jesus' sufferings and prayers were components of His learning during His life on earth.

How does it affect your view of Christ to know that He learned obedience through His suffering?

In the Hebrews 5 passage underline all the words that describe Jesus' humanity. Circle the elements that speak to His divinity.

How does this text inspire you to pursue a vibrant prayer life?

It's striking that throughout the Gospels we see Jesus praying. His prayer life is especially highlighted in the Gospel of Luke. Read the following examples and record any observations you have about Jesus' prayers.

At His baptism:

> When all the people were baptized, and when Jesus also had been
> baptized and was praying, the heavens were opened, and the Holy
> Spirit descended on him in bodily form, like a dove; and a voice came
> from heaven, "You are my beloved Son; with you I am well pleased."
> **LUKE 3:21-22**

As the crowds continually sought to find Him:

> The report about him went abroad, and great crowds
> gathered to hear him and to be healed of their infirmities.
> But he would withdraw to desolate places and pray.
> **LUKE 5:15-16**

Prior to choosing the disciples:

> In these days he went out to the mountain to pray, and all night
> he continued in prayer to God. And when day came, he called his
> disciples and chose from them twelve, whom he named apostles.
> **LUKE 6:12-13**

When He was transfigured before some of the disciples:

> About eight days after these sayings he took with him
> Peter and John and James and went up on the mountain
> to pray. And as he was praying, the appearance of his face
> was altered, and his clothing became dazzling white.
> **LUKE 9:28-29**

When His disciples asked Him how to pray:

> Jesus was praying in a certain place, and when
> he finished, one of his disciples said to him, "Lord,
> teach us to pray, as John taught his disciples."
> **LUKE 11:1**

On the eve of His crucifixion:

> Being in an agony he prayed more earnestly; and his sweat became like
> great drops of blood falling down to the ground. And when he rose from
> prayer, he came to the disciples and found them sleeping for sorrow.
> **LUKE 22:44-45**

Based on these texts, what's your general impression about the role of prayer
in Jesus' personal spiritual life?

As you've examined these texts, what patterns in Jesus' prayer life do you need
to establish in your own prayer life?

If the Lord Jesus needed to pray, how much more do we, who are being perfected in Christ, need to pray? Unlike us, Jesus wasn't being perfected from a sin nature; He was merely maturing in His already perfected state of perfection. He relied on prayer for this process.

Charles Spurgeon included two chapters on prayer in his classic *Lectures to My Students*. In the chapter titled "The Preacher's Private Prayer" he urged that a preacher's prayer life should show itself in life and ministry. Spurgeon argued that an effective preaching ministry flows from a sanctifying life wrought through prayer. In the mind of Spurgeon, to neglect prayer is to neglect accessing God, who has promised spiritual growth for the preacher and his hearers. I would argue that not just the preacher but all God's people need to find their strength for growth, life, and ministry in prayer.

Read these words of Spurgeon, assuming they apply to all Christians:

> Of course the preacher is above all others distinguished as a man of prayer. He prays as an ordinary Christian, else he were a hypocrite. He prays more than ordinary Christians, else he were disqualified for the office which he has undertaken. "It would be wholly monstrous," says Bernard, "for a man to be highest in office and lowest in soul; first in station and last in life." Over all his other relationships the preeminence of the pastor's responsibility casts a halo, and if true to his Master, he becomes distinguished for his prayerfulness in them all. As a citizen, his country has the advantage of his intercession; as a neighbor those under his shadow are remembered in supplication. He prays as a husband and as a father; he strives to make his family devotions a model for his flock; and if the fire on the altar of God should burn low anywhere else, it is well tended in the house of the Lord's chosen servant—for he takes care that the morning and evening sacrifice shall sanctify his dwelling.[1]

In what ways is it hypocritical for Christians not to pray?

What does it say about our faith if prayer isn't a central feature of our walk with God?

What changes do Spurgeon's words encourage you to make in your prayer life?

There's a pitfall we all face with our prayer—something that can sidetrack us in our desire to grow through prayer. This pitfall is a habit of complaining. It prevents us from developing the prayer life we seek. It's easy to complain; it's difficult to faithfully pray.

We complain about what we don't have, our jobs, our children, our spouse or our singleness, our church, our neighbors, and our cities. But we don't recognize prayer as the catalyst of change from God.

Too often we complain about what's wrong with the church instead of praying for change by the Holy Spirit. Do you think your church is dysfunctional? Read Paul's letters to the church in Corinth. Paul had plenty to complain about, and though he rebuked the church, he never failed to pray for it. Read some of Paul's prayers for that church:

> I give thanks to my God always for you because of the grace of God
> that was given you in Christ Jesus, that in every way you were enriched
> in him in all speech and all knowledge—even as the testimony about
> Christ was confirmed among you—so that you are not lacking in any
> gift, as you wait for the revealing of our Lord Jesus Christ, who will
> sustain you to the end, guiltless in the day of our Lord Jesus Christ.
>
> **I CORINTHIANS 1:4-8**

> We pray to God that you may not do wrong—not that we may appear
> to have met the test, but that you may do what is right, though
> we may seem to have failed. For we cannot do anything against
> the truth, but only for the truth. For we are glad when we are
> weak and you are strong. Your restoration is what we pray for.
>
> **2 CORINTHIANS 13:7-9**

Paul was intentional about praying for the church and for sanctification to take place in the lives of believers. He constantly encouraged them and reminded them to rely on the gospel and God's grace as the basis for being restored to fellowship with God, for being sanctified in the likeness of Jesus, and for growing in their prayer lives.

Paul had a tumultuous relationship with the Corinthian church. How do his prayers inspire you to pray for people with whom you've difficult relationships?

Jesus called us to pray for people who persecute us (see Matt. 5:44). To some degree Paul was doing this for the Corinthians. How often do you do this in your prayer life? How can you move forward in this area?

When we face challenges in our spiritual lives, as these believers did, it does us no good to try and solve our problems alone. We lack the power to change. We need to pray and ask God for His will to be done and for Him to change our hearts and minds. He knows better than we do the changes that need to take place in our lives. Praying for the will of God means praying for the implications of the gospel to be applied to issues in our lives that need to be transformed.

Prayer isn't dictating our will to God but aligning our will with His will. God uses prayer to grow us. As we spend time in prayer, God melts us and molds us into His Son's image. As we spend time in the presence of God in prayer, we find ourselves praying what we wouldn't have prayed before.

It's awesome to think we have access to God through Jesus Christ. We must take advantage of this powerful opportunity that's afforded only to the redeemed. To unleash God's sanctifying power in our lives, we must pray in faith, by the power of the Spirit, for the alignment of our will with the will of Christ, to whose image we're being conformed.

Finish this section of study by praying this prayer.

Dear Lord, I pray that You'll make everything I've learned about sanctification through prayer sink down deep into my heart. Help me become a person who prays. I pray that my friends and family members will see me as an example of someone who draws close to You through prayer on a consistent basis. Lord, I want to be sanctified. I want You to mold me into Your image, and I know a healthy prayer life is critical for that to happen. I confess that I've repeatedly fallen short in this area, and I humbly ask You to change me by Your Holy Spirit. I can't change on my own. My sanctification is in Your hands, and I submit myself to that process. I love You, Lord, and I pray that my prayer life will reflect my love for You. Amen.

1. Charles Spurgeon, *Lectures to My Students* (New York: Sheldon & Company, 1875), 66.

Prayer isn't dictating our will to God but aligning our will with His will.
#UNLEASHED

OVERCOMING STRONGHOLDS

START

As you completed this week's personal study, what did the Lord show you? How did He speak to you?

Have you ever heard the term *stronghold* before? What's your impression of it?

What are you hoping for in this final session of *Unleashed?*

In the Old Testament the people of Israel often struggled with idolatry, worshiping other gods instead of the one true God who'd saved them from slavery in Egypt. The people built altars to these other gods, and these strongholds stood as physical monuments to ideologies that were opposed to God. Although we as Christians don't worship other gods or goddesses at physical altars today, we're vulnerable to the same sorts of alternative mindsets and value systems that stand opposed to Christ. These mindsets and value systems are strongholds, and they can warp our view of God and impair our ability to follow Christ and maintain a biblical view of the world. Strongholds are much bigger than any individual sin because they permeate our minds and skew our thinking about who God is and about His will for our lives.

Today we'll hear Pastor Mason describe the nature of strongholds and explain how we can make sure they don't take root and hinder our spiritual growth.

Watch video session 6, in which Pastor Mason addresses the tough, ever-present reality of spiritual strongholds.

WATCH

Though we walk in the flesh, we are not waging war according to
the flesh. For the weapons of our warfare are not of the flesh but
have divine power to destroy strongholds. We destroy arguments
and every lofty opinion raised against the knowledge of God,
and take every thought captive to obey Christ, being ready to
punish every disobedience, when your obedience is complete.

2 CORINTHIANS 10:3-6

The angel of the LORD came and sat under the terebinth at Ophrah,
which belonged to Joash the Abiezrite, while his son Gideon was
beating out wheat in the winepress to hide it from the Midianites.
And the angel of the LORD appeared to him and said to him, "The
LORD is with you, O mighty man of valor." And Gideon said to him,
"Please, sir, if the LORD is with us, why then has all this happened to
us? And where are all his wonderful deeds that our fathers recounted
to us, saying, 'Did not the LORD bring us up from Egypt?' But now
the LORD has forsaken us and given us into the hand of Midian."

JUDGES 6:11-13

That night the LORD said to him, "Take your father's bull, and the
second bull seven years old, and pull down the altar of Baal that your
father has, and cut down the Asherah that is beside it and build an altar
to the LORD your God on the top of the stronghold here, with stones
laid in due order. Then take the second bull and offer it as a burnt
offering with the wood of the Asherah that you shall cut down."

JUDGES 6:25-26

RESPOND

In this session Pastor Mason addressed the difficult subject of spiritual strongholds. We all have the capacity to allow strongholds to take root in our lives.

What stood out to you about Pastor Mason's teaching?

Have you ever had an experience with a spiritual stronghold? What did God show you through that experience?

What did you find interesting or challenging about Gideon's story?

As Pastor Mason said, many strongholds are not the obvious ones we might think of—for example, adultery or an addiction to pornography. A stronghold can be any mindset that sets it up against the gospel of Jesus Christ.

What strongholds do you think our culture tolerates or promotes?

What strongholds do you think are especially risky for our families? For our churches?

What did you find most challenging in this session?

In closing, pray and ask God to show you whether there are any strongholds in your life that need to be torn down and replaced with the truth of Christ. Then ask Him to give you strength to submit to His sanctifying work in that area.

Complete the following three personal-study sections to conclude this study. One section will focus on this week's big idea, the next section will dig deeper into Scripture, and the final section will focus on application.

THE BIG IDEA

Spiritual strongholds. Everyone has them, but we all tend to minimize them. They're our greatest impediment to sanctification because they affect what we believe about faith in God and His Word. Strongholds bind us to the world rather than to the greatness of the growth that the Lord has planned for us. Let's get unleashed from our strongholds.

What's a stronghold? Our core passage for addressing strongholds is 2 Corinthians 10:3-6:

> Though we walk in the flesh, we are not waging war according to
> the flesh. For the weapons of our warfare are not of the flesh but
> have divine power to destroy strongholds. We destroy arguments
> and every lofty opinion raised against the knowledge of God,
> and take every thought captive to obey Christ, being ready to
> punish every disobedience, when your obedience is complete.
>
> **2 CORINTHIANS 10:3-6**

According to Paul, strongholds are fleshly arguments that resist the Word of God. Strongholds compete in our minds with God and His Word. They're systems of unbelief that inhibit our ability to grow through the sanctifying work of the gospel of Christ by faith. In other words, strongholds cause us to have a faithless faith or an unbelieving belief.

Go back and reread the previous Scripture passage. In your own words describe how spiritual strongholds work in a person's life.

What actions do the verses give believers for fighting strongholds in their lives?

A stronghold isn't necessarily a particular outward sin but a sinful mindset that creates an environment for sin. A classic example of a stronghold is the rebellious attitude the people of Israel had during the period of the judges. The Book of Judges ends on an ominous note: "In those days there was no king in Israel. Everyone did what was right in his own eyes" (Judg. 21:25).

The people of Israel had a mindset that caused them to engage in sinful patterns of behavior. This mindset was a self-centered viewpoint. The people of Israel did what they thought was right. They were their own standard of truth instead of God.

> **Reflect on a period in your life when you habitually did what was right in your own eyes. What was that period like?**

> **How would you describe your view of God during that period?**

> **What was your relationship with God like during that time?**

In the Old Testament a negative stronghold was commonly a physical, fortified place of idolatry, an altar or a sanctuary dedicated to worshiping a god or goddess. The idolatry connected to these strongholds represents, both literally and figuratively, what happens when the people of God replace God and His Word with idols. Instead of having faith in God, the Israelites placed it elsewhere. Isn't that true of us today?

My working definition of *stronghold* is *a mindset, value system, or thought process that hinders your spiritual growth and your ability to exalt Jesus above everything in your life.*

> **Spend a few moments in reflection. Identify any strongholds you may be currently experiencing in your life. How are they working to distort the truth about God and to stunt your spiritual growth? Record your thoughts in the columns.**

Current Strongholds	Lies They Communicate

What strongholds do you see in our culture today—structures that are set up as rivals to God's truth, like altars to false gods in the Old Testament?

David Wilkerson's thoughts are helpful in clarifying the meaning of a spiritual stronghold:

> A stronghold is an accusation planted firmly in your mind. *Satan establishes strongholds in God's people by implanting in their minds lies, falsehoods and misconceptions, especially regarding God's nature.* For instance, the enemy may plant in your mind the lie that you're unspiritual, totally unworthy of God's grace. He may whisper to you repeatedly, "You'll never be free of your besetting sin. You haven't tried hard enough. You haven't changed. And now God has lost patience with you because of your continual ups and downs."[1]

What's your reaction to Wilkerson's explanation of a stronghold?

Have you ever felt that a lie had been planted in your mind? If so, what was it, and how did it affect your relationship with Christ?

Most of the sinful habits I help people deal with in ministry are rooted in strongholds. Shepherding people through these issues requires them to face the roots of their strongholds and to exalt Jesus above them. In all of our lives (including mine), strongholds create blind spots that keep us chained to earth instead of heaven.

There are three types of strongholds: personal, family, and cultural. These are fortified places of fleshly thinking that hold us hostage to sin and impede our spiritual growth in those areas.

PERSONAL STRONGHOLDS

Personal strongholds are areas of bondage that are reinforced by our personal nurturing. These are bad mindsets that have been nurtured by our fallen affections. They often take the form of emotional strongholds, including anger, depression, bitterness, and disappointment. With personal and emotional strongholds, we tend to focus on past circumstances rather than our belief in what God's Word says about our identity.

For example, if a young person is repeatedly abused sexually and the deep pain it causes is never addressed biblically, a stronghold will form. Molestation is a heinous sin, and its effects on our emotions can cause us to formulate a stronghold in our response to that experience. The Enemy will throw lies at us like "God isn't good! Where was He all those years? He doesn't care about you! You're worthless!"

Victims of abuse are then tempted to nurture a false theology of God and their identity in Christ, based on sin that's been perpetrated against them. They can develop a system of belief that affects every area of their lives, exacerbating the pain they experienced. Emotional scars are real and can give birth to spiritual strongholds later in life. These long-term effects are one reason abuse is so evil.

Have you experienced any personal strongholds, or have you seen a family member experience one?

What was the impact on your faith or on your family member's faith?

Paul's words in Galatians 2 can introduce truth to someone trapped in a personal stronghold:

> I have been crucified with Christ. It is no longer I who live,
> but Christ who lives in me. And the life I now live in the flesh I live
> by faith in the Son of God, who loved me and gave himself for me.
> **GALATIANS 2:20**

How could this verse help someone struggling with a personal stronghold?

FAMILY STRONGHOLDS

Among the fiercest strongholds I've seen are family strongholds. All families are dysfunctional, but spiritual dysfunction results when unbiblical patterns emerge in a person's life because of family. If a family doesn't deal with issues biblically, the way family members respond to problems and challenges will be affected for the rest of their lives.

One element I instituted in our premarital class at Epiphany Fellowship Church is a session on family history. As part of the training, each couple must write down the positive and negative qualities of their parents or guardians. We don't do this to place unfair scrutiny on parents but to help members understand themselves more fully before forming a new family. After the exercise is complete, participants must ask someone who knows them well what characteristics or issues they see in their lives. Many are shocked by how often the negative traits they assigned to their parents are manifested in their own lives. Family strongholds, for the most part, are strongholds a family holds in common.

Can you think of any sinful attitudes or behaviors that have been common to your family or have appeared through several generations?

Do you know why this stronghold appeared in the first place?

What characteristics of this stronghold do you see in your life? If you don't see any, how can you guard your life against them?

CULTURAL STRONGHOLDS

Cultural strongholds are beliefs and practices that people groups hold in common as normal but are antithetical to the gospel. These people groups can be ethnic, socio-economic, geographic, or another type of group. Although these strongholds are widely accepted by those who belong to the culture, they must be challenged and destroyed.

I grew up in an environment in the post–civil-rights era when every message from the pulpit was racially charged. I grew up around black nationalists who saw a conspiracy everywhere, and I went to one of the oldest historically black colleges in the country during a time when hip-hop artists had an activist edge to their craft. My parents grew up in the Jim Crow South. I grew up in D.C. in the crack era. My response to this cultural background was to develop an unbiblical framework for thinking about God and the world around me.

Cultural strongholds are some of the hardest to break because if they're shared by others in the culture, they can be rationalized through consensus. Even early Christian leaders like Peter and Barnabas faced cultural strongholds. For example, Paul described a confrontation with Peter and Barnabas in Galatians 2:

When Cephas came to Antioch, I opposed him to his face, because he stood
condemned. For before certain men came from James, he was eating with
the Gentiles; but when they came he drew back and separated himself,
fearing the circumcision party. And the rest of the Jews acted hypocritically
along with him, so that even Barnabas was led astray by their hypocrisy. But
when I saw that their conduct was not in step with the truth of the gospel,
I said to Cephas before them all, "If you, though a Jew, live like a Gentile
and not like a Jew, how can you force the Gentiles to live like Jews?"

GALATIANS 2:11-14

What's going on in this passage? Peter (called Cephas here, the Aramaic version of Peter) came to visit Paul and the Christians in Antioch. Because of the unifying nature of the gospel, he freely ate with Gentiles. But when Jews came from Jerusalem to visit, Peter wouldn't eat with the Gentiles because he feared what the Jews would think of him. Barnabas fell into the same trap, and Paul called them out on it.

Identify any cultural strongholds like this—attitudes, behaviors, or ideologies
that run counter to the gospel.

How have you been able to distance yourself from cultural strongholds?
If you haven't, what steps will you take to do so?

Finish this section of study by praying that the Lord will help you identify and
overcome any personal, family, or cultural strongholds in your life that limit
your spiritual growth.

1. David Wilkerson, "Dealing with Our Strongholds," *David Wilkerson Devotions* [online], 23 July 2009 [cited 4 December 2015]. Available from the Internet *http://davidwilkersontoday.blogspot.com*.

*Strongholds bind us to the world rather
than to the greatness of the growth
that the Lord has planned for us.*
#UNLEASHED

DIGGING DEEPER

No matter how deeply bound we are to any given stronghold, through Jesus Christ we're able to overcome it. Christ is mightier than the most stubborn heart and the greatest lie of Satan. On the cross Jesus disarmed Satan's devices and conquered every fear and hurt through His love for us (see Col. 2:8-15). Christ is mighty enough to redirect our sin-rich hearts heavenward so that we can get back on the track of spiritual growth.

In the Book of Judges we see an unrighteous generation rise up among God's people. God had provided comforts for the previous generation, and unfortunately, the new generation responded in a way that caused them to become nominal in their commitment to the Lord. When a generation arises that hasn't been diligently shepherded in the Word of God, strongholds will follow.

In Judges 6 a man named Gideon had an encounter with God that changed the trajectory of his life. In verses 11-32 we witness the almost immediate transformation of a life by God when His servant properly confronted a stronghold.

> Take a moment and read Judges 6, paying special attention to verses 11-32. We'll come back to this passage, so keep your Bible open to this text.
>
> What stood out to you about this text? What spiritual strongholds did you see?
>
> What lie did Gideon believe about God (see v. 13)? Have you believed this same lie? How have you responded to it?
>
> What altars to false gods do you need to tear down in your life?

Appearing as an angel, God confronted Gideon's stronghold (see v. 11). God made the move toward Gideon; Gideon didn't move toward God. A wonderful fact about our great God is that He's willing to engage us even when we refuse to engage Him.

God sat under a tree and watched Gideon beat wheat in the winepress. This is unusual, because ancient people usually threshed their grain on hilltops in order to take advantage of the wind that would separate the wheat from the chaff. However, because threshing the wheat in the open would have aroused the attention of the marauding Midianites, Gideon resorted to beating the grain under an oak in a sheltered vat used for pressing grapes, making his work much harder. By working in the winepress, Gideon used for one purpose something meant for another purpose.

I call this misuse functional dysfunction. Functional dysfunction results when we're so spiritually blind that we no longer see the strongholds in our lives. We go on working as if nothing's wrong, learning how to cope by functioning in the midst of gross dysfunction. For example, when people struggle with hoarding, they often don't recognize their problem. The intervention of loved ones is usually necessary to help them see the dysfunction they're living in.

Have you ever seen someone living in a stronghold without knowing it? How did it seem to affect their lives?

We're all at risk of allowing a personal, family, or cultural stronghold to take root in our lives. What other examples of functional dysfunction can you think of that defy God's truth and seek to interfere with His desire for our lives?

Gideon's question to God might resemble the responses of many of us who are stuck in strongholds:

> Please, sir, if the LORD is with us, why then has all this happened to us? And where are all his wonderful deeds that our fathers recounted to us, saying, "Did not the LORD bring us up from Egypt?" But now the LORD has forsaken us and given us into the hand of Midian.
> **JUDGES 6:13**

What do you think Gideon was saying about God in this passage?

What cultural stronghold was Gideon verbalizing?

In essence Gideon was asking four questions in this verse:

1. Where's God?
2. Why are we suffering?
3. What happened to God's great power?
4. Why does it seem that the Lord doesn't care for us any longer?

It's interesting that Gideon blamed God for the condition of the people. But in fact, it was all their fault. Their disposition toward the Lord had created the trials they were facing.

Many of us question God because of our circumstances rather than questioning our hearts. When functioning within dysfunction, we might have difficulty perceiving God's promises. But we shouldn't question God's faithfulness if we're trapped in a stronghold; it's far more likely that something else lurks beneath the surface. Many times when we're feeling the effects of our sin, we find ourselves blaming God and others for conditions we've created ourselves.

Reread the four questions Gideon asked God. Which one do you struggle with most? When things get difficult, which question do you default to and why?

The existence of an unacknowledged stronghold doesn't prevent the God of all mercy from pursuing us. God met Gideon in his stronghold. God didn't wait for Gideon to get it right before He pursued him; He pursued Gideon because He knew Gideon couldn't get it right on his own.

In the same way, we're helpless to abandon our sin without God's work in our lives. This is how God demonstrates His love for us. He sent Jesus before our justification, and our sanctification works the same way. God moves to intervene in our brokenness. He takes the initiative. This is the truth Paul was getting at in Romans 5:

> While we were still weak, at the right time Christ died for the ungodly.
> For one will scarcely die for a righteous person—though perhaps
> for a good person one would dare even to die—but God shows his
> love for us in that while we were still sinners, Christ died for us.
> **ROMANS 5:6-8**

Paul said Christ died for the ungodly at "the right time" (v. 6). According to this passage, why do you think it was the right time for Christ to die?

What were we like when Jesus died for us?

How does our salvation in Christ give us victory over strongholds?

Let's return to Gideon's story. How in the world could God refer to a man who was hiding from his enemies and functioning in functional dysfunction as a "mighty man of valor" (Judg. 6:12)? The answer lies in the fact that God doesn't call us to Him based on who we are but on who He is. He sees traits and abilities in people that they don't even see in themselves. God wanted Gideon to know that what He was doing originated with Him.

Our great and mighty God utilizes His résumé, not ours, when He calls us to discipleship and service. God's passion to use us is wrapped up not in our greatness but in His. In Scripture He sometimes went on a holy rant to remind His people who He was. He said this to the people of Israel:

> It was not because you were more in number than any other people that
> the LORD set his love on you and chose you, for you were the fewest of
> all peoples, but it is because the LORD loves you and is keeping the oath
> that he swore to your fathers, that the LORD has brought you out with a
> mighty hand and redeemed you from the house of slavery, from the hand
> of Pharaoh king of Egypt. Know therefore that the LORD your God is
> God, the faithful God who keeps covenant and steadfast love with those
> who love him and keep his commandments, to a thousand generations.
> **DEUTERONOMY 7:7-9**

What does this passage tell you about God?

What does it tell you about the people of Israel and, by extension, about us?

What spiritual stronghold might this passage be addressing? Have you ever struggled with that stronghold in your life?

To see prime examples of the way God can call us out of our dysfunction and make us useful to Him, look at Jesus' world-changing, disciple-making roster. Jesus called religious skeptics, businessmen, Hebrew fundamentalists, thieves, thugs, a shady government worker, radical Jews, mama's boys, spoiled rich kids, prostitutes, outcasts, aristocrats, legalists, and licentious people into one crew to represent Him. What makes the gospel narrative of our lives so great isn't anything we've done but all He's done.

When I used to hit the basketball courts, either I'd go with a solid crew who could play, or I'd wait and choose the good players from the losing team. My desire was to run the court as long as possible with one team. God, on the other hand, goes to the court of life and scouts the players with absolutely no potential. He chooses losers, slow players, poor shooters, and folks who never hustle. But after choosing them to be on His squad, He gives them what they need for the game of life. He receives more glory by winning with that team than with NBA all-stars.

How does it make you feel to know that God chooses unlikely, seemingly unqualified people to carry out His will? What does it tell you about Him?

Read the following passages from Paul's letters to the church in Corinth. Briefly identify the resources God provides in the midst of our weakness.

1 Corinthians 1:26-29

2 Corinthians 12:9-10

How can you yield more control to God in your life and trust Him to work through your dysfunction and weakness?

One of the greatest freedoms in being a Christian is the freedom to deal with our issues head-on. We can see that dealing with our strongholds is a powerful grace from the living God that we need to recognize and engage. Because Christ has already dealt with our bondage to sin, we're promised the power of His victory over any strongholds in our lives. Weakness is no obstacle for God. In fact, He chose you in the midst of your weakness. Rely on God's power to overcome the most powerful strongholds in your life.

Have no fear. Confront your strongholds in the confidence of the victory that Jesus has already won.

Finish this section of study by praying this prayer:

Dear Lord, help me remember the account of Gideon and be inspired by its truth. Help me remember that I may be stuck in a stronghold and not know it. Help me recognize that You're the One who pursues me, not the other way around, so You've already brought me into a relationship with Yourself through the sacrifice of Your Son, Jesus. Please help me identify lies I'm living that are birthed in strongholds and are preventing me from growing in Christlikeness. When You show me strongholds in my life, help me remember and embrace the gospel as the power that will enable me to break free. I submit to Your sanctifying work in my life, including in the process of expelling any strongholds from my heart. Amen.

Christ is mightier than the most stubborn heart and the greatest lie of Satan.
#UNLEASHED

GOSPEL APPLICATION

Breaking a stronghold requires not only personal breakthroughs but also community breakthroughs. A central way we as believers grow into the image of Jesus is through the local church. In this is environment strongholds can be prevented and broken.

In the New Testament it's clear that God uses the church as the primary tool for conforming believers to the image of Christ. You'll never fully unleash the transformative, Spirit-driven power of gospel growth in your life apart from a proper understanding of and love for the local church.

> How would you rate your involvement in church at this point? Mark a representative point on the scale.

1	2	3	4	5
None				Consistent attendance, serving, and giving

> Have you felt your church's support as you've sought to grow in your faith? Why or why not?

> In what ways has your church helped you confront strongholds in your heart?

Biblical community is the interweaving and sharing of life in Christ with the body of Christ. Biblical community is the context in which the church's connectedness to one another gives birth to transformation. Through both accountability and encouragement, we're conformed to the image of Christ. Paul talked about this process in Colossians 3:

> Let the word of Christ dwell in you richly, teaching and admonishing
> one another in all wisdom, singing psalms and hymns and
> spiritual songs, with thankfulness in your hearts to God.
> **COLOSSIANS 3:16**

When Paul says "dwell in you richly," *you* is plural in the original Greek. What does that fact tell you about the role the church plays in our sanctification?

The word *admonish* means *to warn or reprimand someone*. How do you think the church's responsibility to admonish one another could help prevent and combat spiritual strongholds?

This verse also emphasizes teaching "the word of Christ." God calls us to honestly confront our brokenness and sin with the truth of His Word, and the church is the place where we receive a steady diet of truth and a community of truth seekers to rally around us. Connection to a local church is the only sustainable way to confront strongholds in our lives—to prevent them in the first place and to keep them at bay.

Take a few minutes to pray about and record ways you can become more involved in your local church. Maybe you need to attend more often. Maybe you need to join a small group or a Bible-study class. Maybe you need to spend more time around other Christians or to serve through your church. Be honest with yourself and take seriously the idea that God wants to use the church as a major means to conform you to the image of Jesus Christ.

I can engage more consistently in the church by:

One common reason we often don't engage with the church about our strongholds is the shame we feel about them. The cross of Jesus Christ is God's commitment to confront us and heal us at the same time. Jesus didn't run from the shame of the cross but toward it so that we wouldn't have to endure it:

> Let us run with endurance the race that is set before us, looking
> to Jesus, the founder and perfecter of our faith, who for the
> joy that was set before him endured the cross, despising the
> shame, and is seated at the right hand of the throne of God.
> **HEBREWS 12:1-2**

Strongholds can be very shameful places in our lives. Because Jesus already engaged these places of deep brokenness and pain in our lives on the cross, we have no embarrassment to fear. We can run to Him for the help we need to overcome our strongholds.

> **In what ways have you felt shame about the strongholds in your life? Have you sought support from the church? Why or why not?**

> **How does the gospel address your shame about the sinful actions in your life?**

The last time I had a cold, it put me out of commission for almost 1½ weeks. I found out that because it came from a virus, there was only so much I could do. Although I blew my nose, drank plenty of liquids, and got rest, I could address only the symptoms of the virus, not the virus itself. The virus was located much deeper than I was able to reach. Therefore, the doctor ordered medication to help my body fight off the virus.

In the same way, when we're dealing with strongholds, we have to go to the root sin. Dealing with a symptom addresses only the surface level of a stronghold, but the virus that feeds the stronghold remains. God empowers us by the Holy Spirit to fight our strongholds, just as medication strikes at the virus level.

Gideon's encounter with the Lord God gave him the confidence necessary to confront his strongholds. God's presence in his life was the medication he needed to follow God's command to tear down the pagan altar—the physical manifestation of a toxic stronghold that had gripped the people of Israel. God is present to help us confront our strongholds. Through the Holy Spirit we can replace unbiblical value systems with a Christian world-view that leads to greater spiritual growth.

> **You've already identified strongholds in your life and the lies they promote. Record them again below, along with gospel truths that can replace them.**

Strongholds and Lies	Gospel Truths

THE VICTORY IS YOURS

Jesus' second coming could be any day. At that time our process of spiritual growth will reach its completion, and we'll be fully saved. We've been justified by faith in Jesus, we're being sanctified by faith in Jesus, and we'll be glorified by faith in Jesus. The doctrine of glorification refers to the consummation of all things, the time when Jesus will place all things under His feet. Glorification is sanctification made complete.

Although Jesus is the King of kings, the distribution of authority, in both the seen and the unseen realms, is deeply fallen. Christ's kingdom is in a state of "already but not yet." *Already* in that He's the King who's sitting enthroned at the right hand of the Father. *Not yet* in that His rule isn't fully realized by His rebellious creation, and we still experience the effects of the fall. However, His kingdom will come, and when it does, all will know that it has arrived. All will know and see Jesus in all His glory (see Rev. 19).

In what ways do you feel the *already* part of God's kingdom at work in your life?

In what ways do you feel the *not-yet* reality of God's kingdom? What do you hope will change about the world and your spiritual life before Jesus returns?

The blessed hope of Jesus' imminent return motivates our continual spiritual growth while we're on earth. Paul spoke of Jesus' two advents in Titus 2:

> The grace of God has appeared, bringing salvation for all people, training us to renounce ungodliness and worldly passions, and to live self-controlled, upright, and godly lives in the present age, waiting for our blessed hope, the appearing of the glory of our great God and Savior Jesus Christ.
> **TITUS 2:11-13**

How do you think this passage relates to our sanctification?

According to these verses, what's God's role in our sanctification, and what's ours?

Spend a few moments reviewing the tools for sanctification you've studied in the past few weeks. How can you use them to demolish strongholds in your life?

FINAL CHARGE

The first advent of Christ occurred with His incarnation. The second advent will be His full return, when He will end the era of our ability to respond to Him by faith and will usher in the eternal state.

I hope this Bible study has equipped you to understand and pursue a process of sanctification so that you can become more like Christ even now in this period of waiting for His return. All the tools of growth presented in this study must be sought by faith in Jesus Christ. When you do so, the Holy Spirit will use them to grow you immensely in the image of Jesus.

When Jesus returns, He will—

- glorify living and sleeping saints (see 1 Thess. 4:13-17; Rev. 20:6);

- eternally punish the enemies of God (see Rev. 19:1-3,11-21; 20);

- judge the fallen nations (see Rev. 19:11-21);

- destroy death and Hades (see Rev. 20:14);

- eternally judge all believing and unbelieving humans (see Rev. 20:4-6,11-13);

- re-create a groaning universe (see Rev. 21–22:5);

- hand the universal kingdom crown to God the Father (see 1 Cor. 15:24);

- be worshiped universally (see Phil. 2:9-11).

And for all this every saint has a front-row seat. Until then let's live for Him by faith in the glorious gospel. Unleash the power of the Holy Spirit to wreck your idols and replace them with God on the altar of your heart. Be conformed to the image of Christ. Amen.

Record a few words about your biggest takeaways from this study. What has influenced you the most? In what ways has the Lord changed you?

Finish your study with this prayer:

Dear Lord Almighty, I thank You so much for everything I've learned through this Bible study. I pray, Lord, that You'll help me view my life as one long story in which You enable me to grow more and more like Jesus. I pray, Father, that a major theme in that story will be my repeated decision to submit to the Holy Spirit's work in my life, even if it's sometimes painful. I ask, Lord, that You'll sanctify me throughout my life—that my life will be one long crescendo of spiritual growth that reaches its apex in the second coming of Your Son, Jesus Christ. Help me never view myself as the primary driver of my growth. Show me how to be humble and to truly repent of my sin. Cultivate in me a desire to know Your Word and to be shaped by it. Help me pray with consistency so that I can more readily discern Your will for my life. Help me engage with my church as I actively fight the strongholds in my heart. I trust You and praise You for all Your work of sanctification in my life. Amen.

Unleash the power of the Holy Spirit to wreck your idols and replace them with God on the altar of your heart.
#UNLEASHED

NOTES

DID YOU LOVE
UNLEASHED?

Maybe it's time to "like" it.

If your group enjoyed the *Unleashed* Bible Study, help us tell the world about it. Take a few moments to tweet, like, post, and otherwise share the love on all your social media channels.

- **Post a comment** about this study at facebook.com/groupsmatter.
- **Recommend *Unleashed*** to your friends and other groups at your church.
- Here are a few **tweets** to consider:

   "My group is unleashed. Check out the new Bible study from Eric Mason. #Unleashed."

   "LifeWay just released a new Bible study from Eric Mason. #Unleashed"

   "Learn how the gospel encourages, convicts, and empowers us to grow in Christlikeness. #Unleashed"

   "Help other believers actively pursue personal holiness. Check out the new Bible study. #Unleashed"

MORE TITLES FROM
ERIC MASON

BIBLE STUDIES

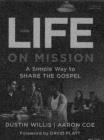

Get everyone in your group on the same page regarding the subject of masculinity. *(6 sessions)*

Learn how to live a missional lifestyle from prominent pastors and authors who live it themselves. *(5 sessions)*

BOOKS

Examine what it means to be a man and how to restore what God intended you to be.

Be comforted and challenged as Eric Mason succinctly articulates God's call of discipleship on every person.